I didn't know what to expect when I first arrived in Hanoi. Made infamous by colonial rule and war, I wondered how Vietnam, still ruled by a Communist government, would be a country open for a loving Christian presence. I learned how. A pastor, over tea, asked his church's government party "watcher" why he was always angry with him. In time, defenses broke, stories were told, and the pastor lovingly embraced one who thought was his enemy. It is in that world that Jacob Bloemberg, as pastor, has learned what it means to love Hanoi. *Love [Your City]* guides us through what it is like to be part of a city movement. It is so elementary in concept yet so profoundly transformative in its outworking. Order copies for your colleagues then begin the process of digesting his story, ready for the Spirit to show you how the love of the Father might be just what your community needs.

Rev. Dr. Brian C. Stiller
Global Ambassador, World Evangelical Alliance
Author, *From Jerusalem to Timbuktu*
General Editor, *Evangelicals Around the World*

Love [Your City] is a blueprint for how a church of any size can be a powerful catalyst for kingdom good in any city in the world. If transformational change can happen in Hanoi, then transformational change can also happen in your city. Drawing from Jeremiah 29:7, his inspirational experience of loving Hanoi and the best and most-current scholarly research on holistic, transformational ministry, Jacob shines the light on the path forward for the Church today.

Dr. Eric Swanson
Director, Leadership Network
Co-author, *To Transform a City* and *The Externally Focused Church*

When Jacob Bloemberg envisioned "Love Hanoi" he wisely merged expatriates and Vietnamese by honoring their love of home country and capital city. By asking the local civic leaders, real needs were identified. Jacob invested and carefully listened then acted and witnessed a city beginning to change. Jacob's overwhelming question 20 years ago was, "How do you do church in the revolving door of the International Church?" When focus shifted from expatriate to national ministry, opportunities emerged exponentially. Expatriates formed a meaningful God-sized purpose to leave a welcomed imprint in Hanoi and Vietnam. Hanoi International Fellowship is doing the Missional International

Church Network vision—reaching a country for Christ by making an authentic, long-term, cross-cultural, significant impact. I'm privileged to introduce my longtime friend and colleague Jacob Bloemberg to you. Have a read! You will want to start loving your city too!

Rev. Dr. Warren Reeve
Founder, Missional International Church Network

In *Love [Your City]*, Dr. Jacob Bloemberg has researched well what it takes to make a citywide impact. This theologically-sound work, laced with amazing life-giving principles, accompanied by years of experience in the city of Hanoi, provides an amazing manual for pastors, teachers, and missionaries. I am confident that the reader will be inspired, not only to move forward on citywide projects, but also will be equipped and inspired to collaborate with others to impact the world they serve.

Pastor Chris Ball
President, Elim Fellowship, NY

What struck me as I read Jacob's story is that what God requires of each of us is availability and obedience. Jacob and his wife demonstrated this from the start. The five core learning steps in this book (the 5 "Ps") outlined are also at the heart of what Micah Global is about, bringing together theology and practice and ensuring the vision we have is towards God's mission. Jacob's experience, of digging into the whole story of God and allowing this to form the framework for the outworking of love for those he was called to serve, reminds us how important it is to be rooted in the Word and to see that nothing is impossible with God. This book shows how God takes ordinary people and does extraordinary things. Dare to imagine the changes God will do as you walk the journey with Jacob in *Love [Your City]*. We have been thrilled to have Jacob share his learning at Micah gatherings and I highly recommend this inspiring book.

Sheryl Haw
International Director, Micah Global

I have followed the Love Hanoi story from when Jacob and I first met at the Urban Shalom summit in Kuala Lumpur, Malaysia, in 2014, and have been impressed by his passion for Jesus, Vietnam, urban mission, and citywide movements. This model of citywide collaboration could be replicated in cities around the world, as churches join together with each other and their neighbors to bring hope and healing to their cities. Jacob's 5 steps to citywide movements can help Christian leaders and mission students from all over the world find ways to love and transform cities. This is a book I think all pastors and missionaries should read, whether they are in the West or the Majority World. Jacob and Linda's story and vision for citywide movements are powerful because they've put the principles in this book into practice for decades. In *Love [Your City]*, Jacob guides us to the biblical principles, missional postures, collaborative practices, and effective processes of transformational urban ministry. This is one of the most important books I've ever read on urban mission and citywide movements.

Dr. Graham Hill
Director, Stirling Theological College, Melbourne
Author, *Global Church* and *Healing Our Broken Humanity*

The world is increasingly becoming an urban landscape. With this evolution comes the challenge of how to share Christ effectively in highly fragmented cities. In this book, Jacob Bloemberg details his experience of Kingdom collaboration in Hanoi, one of the world's most challenging cities. *Love [Your City]* is essential reading for anyone seeking real and tangible spiritual breakthroughs. I heartily recommend it.

Phill Butler
Founder, Intercristro, Interdev, and visionSynergy
Author, *Well Connected*

LOVE❤
[YOUR CITY]

LOVE ♥ [YOUR CITY]

5 STEPS TO CITYWIDE MOVEMENTS

JACOB BLOEMBERG

WESTBOW
PRESS®
A DIVISION OF THOMAS NELSON
& ZONDERVAN

WestBow Press books may be ordered through booksellers or by contacting:

WestBow Press
A Division of Thomas Nelson & Zondervan
1663 Liberty Drive
Bloomington, IN 47403
www.westbowpress.com
1 (866) 928-1240

ISBN: 978-1-9736-8348-3 (sc)
ISBN: 978-1-9736-8347-6 (e)

Print information available on the last page.

WestBow Press rev. date: 02/06/2020

This book is dedicated to my wife Linda:
We first fell in love with each other,
then together we fell in love with Hanoi!

"Seek the shalom of the city
to which I have sent you,
and pray to the Lord for it,
for in the shalom of the city
you will have shalom."
Jeremiah 29:7
(paraphrase mine)

CONTENTS

FIGURES

TABLES

FOREWORD

In my first reading of this book, I found myself in awe at the audacity of Jacob in action over 22 years in the capital city of a country that defeated the United States in what they called "The American War." But then I realized that I had seen this same scenario on my visits to the toughest Red Light districts and urban drug centers in six continents. I delighted in calling YWAM the "urban Wycliffe translators" because they went straight for those urban centers and turned them into training centers. This book has the DNA of YWAM radical spirituality all over it.

By the third reading of this book with my theological educator's glasses on, I realized that the world needs to know HOW Jacob learns and not just WHAT he knows.

Readers should be careful not to rush to the 5-step process. Instead, they should internalize it, which might lead to other programs or even more steps in other cities. Follow Jacob's journey. Identify the process that sustained him for the end game was not seen at the beginning. You will discover that he was re-equipping himself in stages on that journey, and it sustained him for more than 20 years of going deep and imbibing on the culture and history of Vietnam. Like Jesus in Mark 3:14, Jacob knows that ministry is both taught and caught.

Maintaining relationships and having peers of all kinds are critical to urban staying power. It's inverse to programmed mission, so common in our time, which has the solution and only waits for the opportunity to launch the program they've been sent to do. They seek to "take the city" in military fashion or go to claim their "market share" of the audience they wish to reach. It's always the outside in game.

George Bernard Shaw once said, "You see things; and you say 'Why?' But I dream things that never were; and I say 'Why not?'" One of my late mentors, the quotable John Stott in the Lausanne movement, said many times: "Leadership begins with vision, and vision begins with a holy discontent with things as they are." A vision—of and then, for the city—is critical, and it begins with immersion in the cities in both testaments, and all the hundreds of ways the Lord God and His priests, poets, prophets and politicians, sometimes separately; more often collaboratively, combined to show God's redeeming and sustaining love for cities in both testaments. The truth is theology of the city is much more than a ministry to or merely in a city.

While serving as a ministry practitioner in cities and a teacher of global urban ministry, Jacob became a voracious reader. He would seek and test out the things he read from peers. Somewhere along the way (although he doesn't say so himself), he has picked up St. Augustine's idea of "pleasing pagans" and acquired the capacity to see Hanoi as a gift of "common graces," even when "saving grace" ministries are highly restricted.

Sometimes the leaders of ministry in the so-called tough or restricted access places, which so often characterizes urban mission, neither executives or funders, fail to see the results they hoped or planned for from a distance, and they are tempted to pull the plug. Imagine what the report of Jesus' three-year public ministry must've looked like, planned since before the foundations of the earth according to Paul (see Ephesians 1). Jesus opts to spend 50% of His short working time with 12 people, carefully called, chosen, and prepared. The result: The CFO sold Him and the CEO denied knowing Him (thrice!), and the rest hid behind a locked door in an upper room in a widow's home in the city. Can you imagine trying to spin that as success in the press room of heaven?

In this book, you will also discover that Jacob did not ignore that battered 100-year-old church that had survived. Every city has those "Lord have mercy" 5th-commandment churches as I call them. They keep the refugees from "praise worship churches, barely alive, and often behind stained glass."

There was a time when these churches were the biggest and the best the kingdom had. But the passage of time and incidence of wars, inside and outside, have taken their toll. *Should we plant our new church beside them and let these old churches die?* Jacob, looking closely inside, sees a Simeon or Anna in Luke 2, who've never left for 86 years. They are being pastored by memories and promises more than by their current pulpit leaders. Jacob, and his little group of outsiders did not hold on to their new power and privilege, but widened their kingdom lens to build the bridges across unequal and potentially hostile, theological, and sociological divides, leading to the citywide consultations and celebrations so a gathering of the Body of Christ could be the harvest of a century of prayer and patience by so many, both seen and unseen. Billy Graham would have agreed that this is what implementing Jesus' prayer truly looks like; the Lausanne Covenant Article 6 in action: "Let us help the whole church, take the whole gospel to the whole world."

God is now clearly bringing all nations into urban neighborhoods in all six continents. The mission fields have shifted from across oceans to across the street. No longer geographically distant, ministry is now culturally distant, and that is the challenge Jacob and his team have come to understand, and the rest of us need to learn from them.

But I hope this book is not the last word from the Hanoi team. I leave them with another challenge; a historical challenge and perhaps a more consequential one going forward.

There is a Vietnam diaspora in several continents. As a long-time professor of biblical, mission and world Christian history, I know the gifts of diasporas can be huge and transformative over time. Jacob has begun to reach out, and I hope that the scattered Vietnamese will get beyond the pain of war, evacuation, and all the tragedies as well as the loss of the country they knew, to take the steps toward those who remained to work with those among the enemies they left behind.

Dr. Ray Bakke
Founder, Bakke Graduate University
Author, *Theology as Big as the City*
Pentecost 2019, Acme, WA USA

ACKNOWLEDGMENTS

This book is the culmination of an impossible dream, considering that I chose the option for vocational training at age 11 so I did not need to read books! A theme during these past few years while working on doctorate and writing comes from Ephesians 3:20-21:

Now to Him who is able to do immeasurably more than all we ask or imagine, according to His power that is at work within us, to Him be glory in the church and in Christ Jesus throughout all generations, for ever and ever! Amen.

Therefore, I acknowledge up front the unimaginable work God has done in my life, my church, and the evangelical community of Hanoi. Much of the time it felt more like trying to keep up with what God was doing. It is my hope that you, the reader, will not be left with the impression that what is reported has been all my doing and leading; rather, I have done my best to follow and serve to the best of my ability together with my fellow laborers in the city and around the world.

In that light, I express my gratitude for the many people who have contributed to this book and to me personally during this season. First, my thanks go to my always supportive and ever-loving wife Linda—what a journey it has been to travel together with you! Second, many thanks to the leaders, staff, and members of Hanoi International Fellowship, past and present, who have supported my journey and some of my crazy ideas. Third, to my dear Vietnamese colleagues in Hanoi: It has been a privilege to serve, shoulder-to-shoulder, with you. Beyond that, in no order of priority, my thanks go to Ray Bakke and the faculty and staff of Bakke Graduate University; to my comrades in the Missional International Church Network; to Eric Swanson, whose story inspired Love Hanoi and guided me along the way; to my coach and friend Keith Webb; to Beng Alba-Jones, my editor who put her heart and passion into the work; and to my family and the many sponsors "back home" who have supported my work throughout the years.

THANK YOU!

INTRODUCTION

From Holland To Hanoi

Then I heard the voice of the Lord saying,
"Whom shall I send? And who will go for us?"
And I said, "Here am I. Send me!"
Isaiah 6:8

The heat and humidity greeted us as we stepped off the plane and set foot on the tarmac of Hanoi's Noi Bai International Airport. It was May 17, 1997, the day of our first arrival in Vietnam as a family and the day before our oldest daughter's third birthday. Four suitcases and four carry-ons had to suffice for our family of four in our move from the West to the East. (We arranged for the rest of our luggage to arrive later.) Our new teammates picked us up and then dropped us off in the old French Quarter of Hanoi at a hostel on Metal Street. The ancient streets with narrow homes were named after the craftsman guilds and the products that were sold on each street. Metal Street today still sells mostly metal products.

I was sweating profusely, not just because of the hot and humid air, but also because I had started to run a fever. By nighttime the fever was so high that I had become delirious. In my nightmare, I envisioned the bed with large teeth, opening its mouth, ready to eat me! Jumping out of bed, I ran to the door and opened it to escape unto the streets. Holding the doorknob, in a spark of clear thought, I realized that if I'd run away, I may never make it back again. I will surely get lost on the old streets of Hanoi at night. Quickly, I shut and locked the door, fled into the bathroom, and hid myself in the bathtub in fetal position.

Unbeknownst to us, I had contracted dengue fever in Kuala Lumpur, Malaysia, right before boarding the plane to Vietnam. My first week in Hanoi was spent suffering from high fever while Linda had to manage caring for our two little toddlers (aside from a three-year-old daughter, we also had a 15-month-old son) at a hostel on Metal Street. Being sick, I wanted comfort food from home, and thankfully, the French colonialists had left the wonderful heritage of baguette bread, butter, and jam. As a European, this hit the spot! A week later, after we moved into our home, I broke out in a red rash starting from toes and fingers until it covered my whole body and itched like a million bee stings. This was the tell-tale sign of dengue fever. Many in Malaysia had died from the dengue outbreak, yet we had no idea the risk I had run during our first week in Vietnam. Welcome to Hanoi!

When I retell this story of our arrival, listeners are often shocked to hear what we endured in our first week. Even I myself wonder why is it that we didn't despair, get angry, or resented our being in Hanoi. Although Linda had visited Hanoi five months prior for the dedication of the orphanage we were to serve at, it was my first exposure to the city, country, and culture. Yet, once I recovered and was able to start exploring the city, I fell in love with the quaint mix of the European and Asian architecture, the baguettes and the rice, the scooters and the cyclos, and the village feel to the nation's capital. Moreover, what sustained us during that horrific week and the many trials and tests over the following decades was our strong sense of God's call to love Hanoi. So, how did a rural Dutch guy with a Pennsylvania-Dutch wife and their two children end up in the capital city of communist Vietnam? Good question!

FROM A FARMING VILLAGE TO A FRIGHTENING CITY

My parents were both raised in Christian homes as part of the Dutch Reformed Church, one more strict than the other. As an infant, I was baptized and throughout my childhood, I faithfully attended Sunday School. My family lived in an old house on a dead-end street on the edge of a farming town called Nootdorp. Dutch farms are quite small, whatever a family can manage by themselves, and there were three farms just on our short street. With my two brothers and neighborhood friends, we often played in the fields, fished along the canals during summer, and skated on the ice in wintertime. Even in my small village, we were considered "country bumpkins" compared to the town folk.

During my elementary years, we would visit the historic city of Delft and Holland's political capital The Hague for shopping. My dad would often argue that "Delft costs money!" He usually was right. When time came for middle school, my brother and I attended a vocational training school in Delft and bicycled the half hour track to the city each day. Two years later, I switched to a vocational school in The Hague to study graphic arts and printing, riding my bicycle one hour each way.

Now I was in the middle of the worst district of the city and part of a class with dropouts from higher education schools. One student was a rockabilly, bragging about his weekly bar fights. Another was a break-dancer and professional graffiti painter, while another sprayed graffiti just to get his name on walls across the city. One was a punk who brought her rat to school. Another was a posh rich kid who flunked his academics. This was the '80s! *What were my parents thinking sending me here!?* I would have never sent my child to school there, yet God used this time to call me to serve Him in the city. One of my classmates became a close friend, yet he delved into the punk scene, got a big mohawk, became an anarchist, started using drugs, and eventually dropped out of school. This had broken my heart deeply and I prayed daily that God would use my little light to shine in such dark places where my friend had ended up.

My first sense of calling came when the leaders of my youth group showed the movie, *The Cross and the Switchblade.* The video told the story of David Wilkerson and the founding of the drug rehab ministry called Teen Challenge in New York City.[1] This exposure to the oppression of drug addiction among teenagers in the USA grabbed my heart. I could not imagine, however, how I could ever be of any help to drug addicts. After all, I was just studying a vocational trade. The group then watched a documentary of a Christian drug rehab called *The Hope* in Dordrecht, The Netherlands. Suddenly, when I heard the distinctive sound of a Heidelberg printing press, my heart started racing. *God could use a skilled graphic technician to help addicts?!* I knew at that moment that God had a special plan to use my vocational skills and serve troubled youth.

My second sense of calling came while reading the book *Living on the Devil's Doorstep* by Floyd McClung.[2] The book tells the story of the McClung family moving from Afghanistan to Amsterdam in order to rescue drug addicts at the start of what was called "the hippy trail." In 1973, Floyd and his team had rented a houseboat behind Central Station and called it *The Ark*. The boat was used to take in lost and troubled young people and to disciple them. The Ark was the founding ministry of Youth with a Mission (YWAM) Amsterdam. The McClung family then decided to move into the Red Light District, a high crime area known for its public display of prostitution. The family's home and their newly-formed ministry called *The Cleft* was right next door to the satanic church! Reading this story, I frequently had to stop as the Holy Spirit flooded me with His love, a brokenness for the lost, and an assurance of His calling. I prayed for the Lord to use me in the world's darkest places like He had used Floyd McClung and David Wilkerson. If Delft and The Hague were bad, Amsterdam was the big bad city, considered the Sodom and Gomorrah of The Netherlands!

Pursuing this strong sense of calling, I completed the Discipleship Training School (DTS) with YWAM Amsterdam in 1989 and joined The Ark, which by then was a building in the city's center. I also worked with YWAM's outreach ministry called Steiger 14, which used the old houseboat for the weekly "Rock & Roll Bible Study" and other events.[a] I became the sound technician for the No Longer Music band. We would go out on the streets during the day and into the nightclubs after midnight to strike up conversations, build relationships, and invite youth to our evangelistic events. It was during these two years on staff that the third sense of calling pointed me in a whole new direction.

FROM HOLLAND TO HANOI

There were several things I had said I never wanted to do: live in the city, become a student, leave Holland to be a missionary, marry an American (or any non-Dutch), and pastor a church. All of these things happened one by one. I now have learned to never say never!

While serving with YWAM in Amsterdam, the concept of the 10/40 Window had just come out was and often promoted during YWAM meetings (see Figure 1). According to the Joshua Project, "The 10/40 Window is the rectangular area of North Africa, the Middle East and Asia approximately between 10 degrees north and 40 degrees north

---

[a] Learn more about Steiger 14's history at www.steiger.org/about-us/history

latitude." This region is "home to the least evangelized countries…four of the world's dominant religious blocs…the largest unreached peoples over one million…the overwhelming majority of the world's least evangelized megacities … [and] the majority of the world's poor."[3]

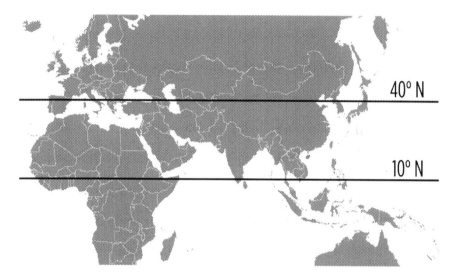

Figure 1: The 10/40 Window Map

My wife Linda had come from the USA in 1990 to work with YWAM in Amsterdam. After completing her DTS, she also moved into The Ark. With a bachelor's degree in Social Work and Psychology, she had felt called to serve the young men and women who had come out of the Red Light district. Before we met, both Linda and I felt a strong call to the 10/40 Window and serve in the most unreached and undeveloped nations. After we married in Amsterdam in 1992, we moved to Elim Bible Institute & College[b] in upstate New York to prepare for a long-term missionary career.

The call to serve in Hanoi came during my second year at Elim. One Sunday morning in October of 1994, while driving to church, Linda and I talked and prayed about our future after graduation. We still felt strongly about serving in a least-reached nation, using our professional skills as substance abuse counselor (Linda) and in graphics and computers (Jacob)

---

[b] Learn more about Elim at www.elim.edu

to help drug addicts and orphans. We prayed and committed ourselves to the Lord, trusting that He would show us where to go and who to go with.

That same week, a missionary candidate came to my class and shared how God had opened the doors for professionals to come to Hanoi, the capital of Vietnam. Irvin Rutherford, his director and founder of Asian Ministry Teams (AMT), had struck an agreement with the government to help orphans, drug addicts, and to do vocational training. In 1972, Rutherford had established Teen Challenge in Saigon, South Vietnam, and his reputation had preceded him. All they needed now were missionaries with vocational qualifications willing to go and serve. I literally jumped out of my seat and asked how I could sign up!

Upon graduation in 1996, we joined Rutherford and AMT in Kansas City, MO, to begin our journey to Hanoi. Irvin was amid raising funds for a new children's home in the city in partnership with the local government. Soon after our arrival, he realized that he also needed to recruit qualified staff to run the program. The agreement with the government specified that AMT would provide an administrator with social work and psychology qualifications. Furthermore, AMT would also provide vocational training for the children. *Here we are, Lord, send us!*

God quickly honored our desire to serve Him. One year after I graduated from Elim, Linda and I with our two children landed at Hanoi's Noi Bai International Airport to work at the Friendship House children's home in Hanoi's Dong Da District. As I've mentioned, our first week was extremely challenging, but after we settled into our home around the corner from Friendship House, life became more adventurous. During our first term of three years, Linda served as the administrator of the children's home alongside our teammates and with the government directors. I became the vocational director and taught the teenagers computer skills while training a few older boys in graphic design. Today, one of those boys has a family of his own and works in the printing industry, designing and publishing printed materials for churches citywide.

FROM MISSIONARY WORK TO MISSIONAL CHURCH

When we arrived, the Hanoi International Fellowship (HIF)[c] was a small congregation of about 30-40 expatriate Christians that met in the Asean Hotel on Chua Boc Street. What had started in a living room by a dozen expat belien vers in August of 1995 continued to grow and moved from one hotel to another. I soon became one of the worship leaders and joined the Steering Committee as the secretary a year later.

In 2003, HIF had hired its first full-time pastor from the USA, but by the end of 2004, came to realize this was not financially sustainable. At the start of 2005, HIF was without a pastor and in a financial and identity crisis. *Was HIF just a club for expatriate Christians who are patting each other on the back, trying to survive yet another week? Or did God have a plan for HIF as a church with a mandate to reach out beyond itself and serve the international community and the city?*

At the same time, I had also experienced a personal crisis in 2003. To gain perspective, I traveled in the region to Laos and Cambodia to discover what God was doing. What I found out was that Christians were integrating business and mission in all kinds of creative ways:

- Missionaries were running handicraft stores to help people with disability
- Two young Americans were running a university funded by the Finnish government
- A Christian NGO ran an English language school to contribute to the nation's development
- A mechanic started a motorbike repair shop as a vocational training program
- An IT guy launched a computer business to do the same

To me this presented a whole new paradigm shift in ministry and missions. I realized that it is the role of the church to equip believers for ministry outside the church and in their places of work. Until then, my focus at HIF had been to recruit and equip believers for church ministry

---

[c] To learn more about HIF, visit www.hif.vn.

only. For the next two years I spent my time researching Marketplace Ministry and Business as Mission and promoting these ideas within HIF. This paradigm shift prepared me for the next major change of focus in our church.

After a season of prayer and fasting at HIF, the leadership and congregation had a strong sense of direction to become more than just a fellowship. We clearly felt called to become an outward-focused international church. Given our dynamic circumstances and sensitive context, the question was, "But how?" To learn more, the chairman and I were sent to attend the Missional International Church Network (MICN) conference in the UAE.[d] Inspired by the vision and language of MICN, we returned with new ideas and a passion to integrate the missional paradigm into HIF's DNA. In August 2005, as HIF celebrated its 10th anniversary, I was appointed as the interim pastor for a six-month period to start implementing this vision. As they say, the rest is history!

I have just told you the short version of my personal journey, of how a Dutch country bumpkin from the rural outskirts of The Hague ended up pastoring an international church in the legendary city of Hanoi, Vietnam. It is and has been an exciting, overwhelming, daunting, and most rewarding journey. The brokenness for the lost, the strong sense of calling, the foundational biblical education, the challenging experiences along the way, and the paradigm shifts that resulted from crisis, all worked together for what God was going to do next. The story I will tell you in the rest of this book was beyond my and anyone else's imagination!

WHO THIS BOOK IS FOR

As I have traveled across the world and shared the Love Hanoi story with individuals, in churches, and at conferences, people react with enthusiasm, surprise, and eagerness to hear more. Local churches in the USA and international churches around the globe want to learn more about how the Love Hanoi journey got started, what inspired me and our church leaders, what the first steps we took were, and how they could possibly start something similar in their city or town. This book is for them and

---

[d] For more information about MICN, go to www.micn.org.

for all those interested to learn more about how to love the city and what God has done in Hanoi.

This book is written for Christian leaders at home or abroad who are passionate about their city and want to start a citywide movement like Love Hanoi. Whether they are church leaders, mission directors, NGO staff, urban practitioners, missionary workers, or non-profit volunteers, God can use anyone to spark a fire. My own personal story illustrates that God will use even someone with vocational training and no desire to leave town or country!

This book is particularly helpful for international church leaders in complicated contexts who scratch their heads in frustration and wonder how their church could possibly become missionally oriented. Trust me, I have been there and done that. Keep in mind, however, that the how is not as important as the why. It is not about copying the answers and replicating the models. As Chapter six will explain further, it is more about the process and asking the right questions. That is what MICN is known for and what helped HIF tremendously in our journey.

You do not need to be a leader to learn from this book. Students of urban ministry, community development, cross-cultural missions, intercultural studies, international relations, and the like will greatly benefit from the ideas, experiences and models presented in this book. As God said through Isaiah, "It is too small a thing ... I will also make you a light of the nations. So that my salvation may reach to the end of the earth" (49:6, NASB). Never settle for thinking too small of what God can do through you! Just serve humbly as you follow the Lord's calling.

How This Book is Laid Out

In response to the requests for information on how to start a similar citywide movement, this book is laid out specifically to help the reader along a 5-step process. This **Introduction, From Holland to Hanoi,** will serve the purpose of helping readers connect personally with my story.

Part One: The Love Hanoi Story, in three chapters, the Love Hanoi Journey will be told, after which I will paint a picture of the history of Hanoi so that the reader gains a better understanding and appreciation of the context. Then the 5-step process to launch a citywide initiative is briefly introduced.

Part Two: 5 Steps to Citywide Movements is divided up into five chapters, which will get into the more nitty-gritty details of each of the five steps.

Chapter 4: Principles, will dive into Scripture to uncover what the Bible has to say about cities and to replace any erroneous beliefs about cities that the reader may have with biblical truths.

Chapter 5: Posture, addresses the issue of the church's attitude towards the city historically and ideally. Just like bad physical posture while working can cramp the body, so a poor social posture can cramp the Body of Christ.

Chapter 6: Process, will introduce several models of approach to transformational urban ministry, including the Missional Process and the Asset-Based Community Development process.

Chapter 7: Partner, expounds on the principles of networking and collaboration across organizational, denominational, and societal boundaries. Special attention will be given to partnering across cultures.

Chapter 8: People, looks at the qualities of transformational leadership needed for each stage of building citywide movements and various models of citywide consultations. The reader will likely be able to identify how they fit into the big picture and who potentially could lead the initiative each step of the way.

Part Three and the final chapter, **Love [Your City] Too!,** will help the reader process how he/she could start a citywide movement initiative. Throughout the book, charts and graphics will help the reader understand the concepts and visualize the ideas (I am a graphic designer after all!).

MY MISSION

It is my desire to help Christian leaders be inspired, theologically-grounded, connected, activated, and to be equipped, so they can increase their missional impact in their community and city. I do this by networking, teaching, writing, preaching, and leading. Christian leaders say I help them see the bigger picture, collaborate with each other, and be equipped with theology and methodologies so they can have a greater missional impact.

Yet, I am only one worker in the field of God's kingdom. Over the decades, together with my wife and numerous teammates, we have plowed, sown, watered, and harvested. It takes many laborers to produce a crop, but only God can make things grow (1 Corinthians 3:7). Therefore, I cannot take any credit for the fruit of my labor, only that God has been faithful to use me as a servant. You also are invited to participate in this global movement of citywide collaboration to love our cities well for the glory of our heavenly Father. To that extent, please use any and all of this book's content to share with others, because the mission is too big to do alone!

PART ONE:

THE LOVE HANOI STORY

CHAPTER 1

LOVE HANOI: THE JOURNEY

Now to him who is able to do immeasurably more than all
we ask or imagine, according to His power that is at work
within us, to him be glory in the church and in Christ Jesus
throughout all generations, for ever and ever! Amen.

Ephesians 3:20-21

It's not fair Lord! This is not America, this is Hanoi! I was frustrated, agitated, upset really, that the Lord let me read another inspiring book from the USA with ideas that were seemingly impossible to implement in my context of Vietnam's capital city, Hanoi. The book *To Transform a City* by Eric Swanson and Sam Williams tells the story of Love Boulder. Pastors from around the city of Boulder, Colorado, had been meeting together to pray for church planting opportunities in that liberal university city, which at time, did not have one evangelical church. The Lord spoke to them with just two words: Love Boulder. "It was not about reaching Boulder, converting Boulder, changing Boulder; it was about *loving* Boulder."[4] The pastors ended up meeting with city leaders and with the mayor, asking them how the churches could help with the urban issues of Boulder, and started collaborating in community development projects, to the glory of our Father in heaven (Matthew 5:16).

I was upset because in Hanoi, unlike in Boulder Colorado, the pastors were not united and meeting to pray for their city. Even if they were, there would not be an opportunity for pastors to meet with the mayor of Hanoi. Even if they could, why would the mayor share with the pastors openly about the issues he is facing? Even if he would, why would he want the help of such a tiny religious minority? Protestant Christians comprised only 0.1% of the city's seven million population then. Vietnam's war had created a deep divide between government and religion, between state and church. My family had arrived in Hanoi in 1997 to work with orphanages through a Christian non-governmental organization. One thing I had learned since then was how limited we as Christians were in Hanoi at that time.

THE BIRTH OF LOVE HANOI

Despite my frustrations, the Love Boulder story inspired the leadership of the Hanoi International Fellowship (HIF) to initiate the Love Hanoi campaign in 2012. Seven years prior, in 2005, I had been called to pastor the church for an interim period. HIF was going through a paradigm shift from being an internally focused fellowship for expatriate Christians to an externally focused international church. At the same time, I joined the Missional International Church Network (MICN) which wrestled with the same question as we did: *How can an international church be possibly missional in a context such as ours?* The missional journey since had prepared me and our church to become a willing partner in citywide collaboration and urban transformation.

I must confess, though, that it was rather accidental than intentional that HIF started the Love Hanoi campaign. The elders of HIF were on a prayer retreat to seek the Lord's direction for the following program year of 2012-13. Getting towards the end of our retreat, the whiteboard was still blank! *What will we tell our congregations? That we heard nothing from the Lord?* Then, one of the elders, who also had read *To Transform a City,* said, "Let's start Love Hanoi!" Though the other team members had not read the book, after being given a brief explanation, they became excited about the idea and chimed in. Thinking it was rather impossible, I nevertheless agreed that we might as well start, even if we had no idea how to go about it and what possibly we could accomplish. Love Hanoi ended up being the only goal on the whiteboard and the only vision we presented during Vision Sunday in May of 2012.

LOVE HANOI'S FIRST STEPS

The first things we did when we returned after the summer holiday was to preach a six-week series titled, *Love Hanoi: Inspired by Nehemiah.* I had enrolled in a doctoral program on city transformation with Bakke Graduate University (BGU) and had started the first course on Practical Urban Theology. Mark Gornik's book published in 2002, *To Live in Peace: Biblical Faith and the Changing Inner City*, included a retelling of Nehemiah's story within the context of community development. Based on Wallace's six events of cultural revitalization, Gornik had outlined the book of Nehemiah in six stages. This provided an outline for HIF's sermon series, though with different titles.[c]

1. Nehemiah 1: What's the news?
2. Nehemiah 2: What's in your hands?
3. Nehemiah 3: Let's build together!
4. Nehemiah 4-6: Don't give up!
5. Nehemiah 7-10: Commit to the community!
6. Nehemiah 11-13: What's next?

A simple logo for Love Hanoi was created and that, combined with a drawing of typical Hanoi houses, became our brand (see Figure 2). We started printing T-shirts, coffee mugs, and other promotional products, which we sold to inspire people to love the city. This also inspired expatriates in the wider community. The Hanoi International Women's Club invited us to have a booth at the annual Christmas Charity Bazaar, which draws thousands of people from all over the city. HIF singers and musicians performed African songs and praise music during the bazaar while wearing the Love Hanoi shirts and became the highlight of the day. We realized that Love Hanoi now had helped build a bridge to the expatriate community. HIF had become known for Love Hanoi among our peers. Over the years, Hanoi's skyline has drastically changed, and

---

[c] For other outlines and retelling of Nehemiah, see *Renewing the City: Reflections on Community Development and Urban Renewal* by Robert D. Lupton and *City of God, City of Satan* by Robert C. Linthicum.

our branding today reflects the modern look of our city while the logo is custom drawn Vietnamese calligraphy (see Figure 3).

Figure 2: Love Hanoi branding 2012

Figure 3: Love Hanoi branding 2016

"How Can We Love Hanoi?"

It was truly God-ordained that we launched the Love Hanoi campaign in 2012, the same year that we started building relationships with city and national government officials. The year before, HIF had launched a second worship service in MyDinh on the western side of the city. HIF was now renting a ballroom at the InterContinental Hotel in Westlake and in the newly opened Crown Plaza in MyDinh, which was costly. In 2012 we were considering moving that congregation, with over 200 people in attendance, into a brand new office building owned by a local Christian. To find out if having a church in an office tower would be permitted, we needed to ask the government. Since HIF was founded in 1995, we had not been given a permit to operate. We also did not have any relationships with government officials.

Our first meeting was with a Colonel from the Protestant office of the religious department of Hanoi's security police. When that went well, he came to visit our worship service at the Westlake location, and was impressed by our casual way of worship compared to Catholic services. Next came an invitation to meet the Colonel's boss, a General, at the city police headquarters. After realizing that we didn't have any hidden agenda and that we simply wanted to help, the General was very appreciative of our desire to love his city and referred us to the social work department, while assuring us that we as foreigners have the freedom to worship in Vietnam.

Over the following years, each time I met with government officials at the city or national level, I would repeat the same question without making any demands. Eventually HIF and Love Hanoi became synonymous. We never did receive verbal or written permission to move into that office building, but we also did not receive a "no" for an answer. In April 2013, our MyDinh congregation and our church offices moved into our first permanent home on the 17th floor of the Detech Tower. In the process, we had even obtained verbal permission to have Vietnamese come to our worship services and "to take good care of their spiritual needs," as I had been told. What an amazing answer to so many prayers of previous decades! Beyond my imagination!

Our posture and our actions to love the city and contribute to society through our Love Hanoi campaign had built bridges with local and national government. Moreover, I personally had overcome my fears of engaging with city police and religious affairs officials because in my relationships with them we have discovered a common interest: to love their city. What HIF's leadership desired next was to see a citywide movement take place among all the churches to love their city in tangible ways.

LOVING HANOI TOGETHER

During Easter of 2014, the Hanoi Evangelical Church (HEC) invited HIF and the Hanoi Korean Church (HKC) to organize a joint Easter concert in a modern theater with over 700 seats. Because we needed police permissions for any outside event, Pastor Paul of HEC invited the Chief of Police to attend. Surprisingly, Major General Nguyen Duc Chung came, together with the head of Hanoi Security Police (like the FBI) and Hanoi Religious Affairs representatives! They enjoyed the cross-cultural performances, stayed for the whole concert, and even gave a donation.

Because HIF MyDinh's site-pastor, Nelson Annan, was planning to return to Canada, we decided to ask the Chief of Police if we could come visit so Nelson could say thank you and goodbye. This led to our first formal visit with the Chief of Police, with Pastor Paul serving as our translator (whose idea it was to begin with and who had made the arrangements). We handed out Love Hanoi products as gifts and received gifts from MG Chung. Not only was I nervous, but I found out later than the uniformed police officers were just as nervous to meet the foreign Protestant Christian delegation. Later that day, the meeting was reported in the online police newspaper with my quote as the title: "Hanoi is safer than my home country" (see Figure 4).[5] Having raised my children in Hanoi, I felt safer than if I had raised them in Amsterdam!

"An ninh ở Hà Nội còn tốt hơn nước tôi"

19:01 29/05/2014 Đào Lê Bình

ANTĐ Sáng nay 29-5, Đoàn mục sư của cộng đồng những người nước ngoài theo đạo Tin lành ở Hà Nội đến chào và trao đổi một số công việc với lãnh đạo Công an Hà Nội.

Figure 4: Shaking hands with the Chief of Hanoi Police

For Capital Liberation Day in October of 2014, we returned to visit the chief at the police headquarters with a delegation of pastors and leaders from HEC, HKC, and HIF. This time, MG Chung gave us a personal tour of the newly-constructed police theater. Then, surprisingly, the chief said that we could come and hold a Christmas concert there after the completion of the construction! *Yeah, right. What Christian would want to come to the police headquarters to celebrate Christmas!?* Other church leaders were concerned about our growing friendship with the city police, yet here we were.

LOVE HANOI CHRISTMAS CONCERT

Meanwhile, HIF organized our own Christmas concert in the public theater. As we had to obtain permits from various government officials, we invited them all to come. MG Chung came along with the head of the security police department, and representatives of religious affairs, department of culture, foreign relations, and district police. This time we felt more comfortable around each other. Since we used the concert to raise funds for charity projects through our Love Hanoi campaign, the national TV reporters who had come reported the following day on the Love Hanoi Christmas Charity Concert—even though that is not what we had called it. Now, Love Hanoi had built a bridge not only with city officials, but also with national TV channels!

One week later, MG Chung called Pastor Paul and invited us to organize a joint concert at the police headquarters. We couldn't call it a Christmas concert, but instead called it a cultural exchange to welcome the new year. HEC, HKC, and HIF presented a variety of performances, singing about Jesus Christ being the light of the world. We alternated with the police cadets, who danced and sang songs about Ho Chi Minh being the light of Vietnam. A choir from an unregistered Christian drug rehab performed as well. The rehab's pastor shared his testimony, asking forgiveness from the police for all the trouble he had caused the police and society—he had been arrested up to 30 times and imprisoned 14 times! It was all great fun and festive, with church leaders and members, police officials and cadets all celebrating together. The following day, the national security news website reported on the "Welcoming the New Year" concert, stating their praise for the Protestant church's Love Hanoi campaign!

Afterwards, in preparation for Lunar New Year, the pastors and leaders of HEC, HIF, HKC, and now also the house churches, went to visit MG Chung in January 2015. This time, however, we went to the great reception room in city hall as MG Chung had been newly-appointed as Hanoi's mayor! We were warmly welcomed by Hanoi's new mayor and spoke our blessings over him and his entourage of city leaders. Just four years prior I had complained to God that it would be impossible for the pastors in Hanoi to unite and to visit the mayor! I realized that not only had we met the mayor for the first time, we had already visited him several times as the Chief of Police and he had attended our Easter and Christmas concerts. How amazing God works!

LOVE HANOI CONFERENCES

During those years, Love Hanoi was owned by HIF and promoted by CityPartners, the local mission ministry of HIF (see Figure 5). As an international church, with the high turnover of expatriates coming through our doors, we had realized it was better for us not to start our own projects, but to partner with existing organizations and support new initiatives. Partnerships with NGOs, charities, churches, social enterprises and others would enable us to connect our financial and human resources with opportunities to give and serve. CityPartners was rebranded and the team stepped up their game by presenting monthly reports during our Sunday worship services and producing a regular newsletter to connect HIFers with our partners.

Figure 5: CityPartners logo

In November 2015, CityPartners organized the first Love Hanoi Conference. The idea was to build our network, connect our partners, and create a bridge between our Christian and non-Christian constituents. Five of our city partners were given platform time to present on a variety of topics. The city partners and topics were:

- Blue Dragon on the plight of street children
- ColorMe on the plight of trafficked women
- UN-Habitat on the issues of housing, public space, and playgrounds
- Hanoi Evangelical Church on neighboring, helping those in need in the church's community
- Pastor Nguyen Duc Trung on the issue of drug addiction

Over 100 people participated from various churches and organizations, including foreigners from HIF. A translation booth with headsets was rented and a translator recruited who could simultaneously translate English to Vietnamese and vice versa. This was the first Christian citywide event of this kind on urban topics and the simultaneous translation contributed significantly to its success. There was a buzz in the room all afternoon, with people connecting and networking across organizational boundaries. In the lobby, snacks and drinks were available as well as Love Hanoi products for sale. Love Hanoi stickers were given out for free to spread our branding and to serve as a daily reminder to love our city. As Blue Dragon and UN-Habitat are non-Christian organizations, it was a great opportunity for them and the churches to be connected to each other. We did not make the conference "churchy" in that we did not have worship music or preaching so that our guests would feel comfortable and more willing to return.

From this experience, CityPartners learned that we had filled a need for such a networking and bridge building event. We also realized that presenters need to be more prepared, to submit their presentations in advance, and that we should have four instead of five topics to give the presenters more time to go into greater depth. Contact information had been collected to build CityPartners' database. We decided to organize a second Love Hanoi Conference during the spring, but this time more focused on a theme. In March 2017, the second conference was held with the theme, *Social Entrepreneurship: Solving social challenges with business solutions.* The presenters were:

1. Marc Stenfert Kroese of Donkey Bakery, who worked with people with disabilities to run a café and to cater for four international schools. Marc used the phrase, "People with Special Abilities" rather than "Disabilities." Marc had brought his blind staff Mr. Hoan to share as well;
2. Bich Nguyen of Solar Serve and Family Business Training from Danang, a recipient of a national social enterprise award;

3. Michael Ong of Tea Talk Café & CoRE Center, together with his staff, who focused on counseling and caring for students and young adults; and

4. Pham Quang Nam, a consultant with knowledge on the legal framework for establishing social enterprises.

This conference turned out to be even more successful with about 150 people who came to learn and network. At the end, a survey was done to gather basic information, gauge the success, and solicit topics for the next conference. The topic of Environment came up several times and was selected for the autumn of 2017 conference. However, due to the busyness with the Festival preparations in 2017, the conference was rescheduled for the autumn of 2018.

100-Year Anniversary Celebration

In 2016, the Hanoi Evangelical Church (HEC) celebrated its centennial anniversary. This was a significant milestone, considering that many of those years the church had existed during wartime and under oppression. The church was founded in 1916 during the French colonial occupation, survived the Japanese World War II subjugation, and lived through the prolonged battle for control over Hanoi between the Viet Minh and the French. When the nation was split between North and South at the Geneva Accord in 1954, hundreds of thousands of Catholics and Protestants went South. This left a small remnant of evangelical Christians in Hanoi with the national denomination split along the DMZ. I have been told that by the end of the so-called "American war," only eight church members were left at HEC.

With the increase in cooperation among evangelical church leaders, HEC decided to invite the whole evangelical community in Hanoi to join in the festivities. We were celebrating not only the start of one congregation, but also the birth of evangelical Protantism[f] in the

_____

[f] Evangelicalism is easily misunderstood. In Vietnam, the word *Tin Lanh* is used for the English word *Evangelical*. The literal translation of *Tin Lanh* means "good news," coming directly from the Greek word *euangelion* meaning the same. *Hoi Thanh Tin Lanh* (Evangelical Church) is used as an overarching term for all Protestant

whole city. This turned out to become a large undertaking, with HEC and the help of many others uncovering the history of their church.[g] In preparation, several lead pastors including myself decided to hold the first conference of what we called the Evangelical Community of Hanoi. About 150 pastors and church leaders gathered in HIF's facility to listen to each other's denominational history. These historical accounts had been documented, printed, and bound, and were distributed on that day. For the first time, the so called "underground churches" went above ground with all their contact details and histories. Unimaginable!

The anniversary day, October 14, 2016, had finally arrived. The official ceremonies and celebrations were held during the morning at HEC with government officials, delegates from churches citywide, and missionaries, young and old, in attendance. In the evening a grand celebration was planned. With the help of our friend and mayor MG Chung, HEC was able to rent the Quang Ngua indoor stadium, with a seating capacity of about 6,000. This was the first time most of the evangelical leaders joined together in organizing a citywide event.[h] Just about every Christian from across Hanoi and guests from across the nation and the world attended. This citywide event was a major milestone in Hanoi's history. At the end, we—pastors on the organizing committee—were so elated that we agreed, "Next year again, but bigger!" Except, we could not imagine how!

---

churches, in contrast to Catholic churches, thus Protestantism and Evangelicalism are interchangeable.

[g] It is important to note that to this day, the HEC church building is the only Protestant church building in Hanoi, a city of almost ten million. The building is getting old and has a seating capacity of 220 chairs. In recent years, HEC added a roof to their courtyard, providing additional seating up to 1,000. Almost all other Vietnamese evangelical churches worship in homes, therefore restricted in size. The Korean church and HIF both have a floor in office buildings, in addition to HIF's hotel ballroom at the Westlake site.

[h] In 2011 the Evangelical Church of Vietnam, both the Southern and Northern denominations, celebrated the arrival of the first Christian & Missionary Alliance missionaries as the birth of the evangelical church in Vietnam. During those festivities, the Quang Ngua stadium also had been used for the celebrations in Hanoi. However, this was organized at a national and denominational level, not as a citywide multidenominational effort.

Love Hanoi Festival

Just one week after the centennial celebration, Pastor Paul of HEC received a phone call from the Billy Graham Evangelistic Association (BGEA). "Would the churches in Hanoi be willing to host a citywide festival next year?" was the question asked by Chad Hammond, BGEA's Asia Director. That week, the king of Thailand had died and to mourn the king's death, no festivals were permitted nationwide for one year. BGEA had two festivals initially planned for Thailand in 2017. Because of this recent development, their teams on the ground had to halt the work.

It did not take long for the denominational leaders and local pastors to form a delegation and visit Yangon, Myanmar, where BGEA was holding a festival that November. The Vietnamese pastors met with Franklin Graham, observed the 60,000 Burmese attending the three-day festival, and witnessed the thousands of people responding to the gospel. They were convinced that BGEA's proposal was the answer to our prayer. Unanimously, the Vietnamese pastors extended the invitation for Franklin Graham and BGEA to come to Hanoi the following year.

By the end of January 2017, the BGEA team from Yangon relocated to Hanoi and moved into an office space on the floor below HIF's facilities. Instead of the three years it takes to prepare a BGEA festival, the team now had only ten months to plan and organize until the main event scheduled for December 8-10, 2017. The BGEA staff would always say that the festival is not about the event, but about the process. Only 10% of the work is the event itself, the tip of the iceberg above the waterline. The other 90% is split between organizing, training, and lead-up activities beforehand, and follow-up and discipleship activities afterwards. Little did we pastors understand how big this process turned out to be! The festival was so much bigger than any of us pastors had imagined or could possibly have done alone. BGEA excels at uniting and equipping the church citywide for kingdom impact.

Two surprises happened as the Festival's vision and structure started to take shape. Although the occasion of the Festival was to celebrate the 500th anniversary of the Reformation, BGEA left it to the pastors to choose a name. Without my input or presence, the local church leaders decided to name the festival "The Love Hanoi Festival" (see Figure 6, "Yêu" meaning "Love"). The pastors jokingly said to each other that I would be excited to hear this, and I was! Although I was thrilled, I also had some reservations. *Do the pastors understand the vision of the Love Hanoi campaign?* Love Hanoi focused on practically demonstrating God's unconditional love through community services. The Love Hanoi vision is to bring the kingdom of God out of the church and into the city. It is the difference between a centrifugal and a centripetal force, an outward focus or an inward one, a kingdom out vs. kingdom in vision. My concern was that the pastors' primary objective would be to bring the people of the city into their churches through verbal proclamation only.

Figure 6: Love Hanoi Festival logo

I was surprised again when the Festival's Senior Leadership Team (SLT) decided to create the Love in Action committee and requested me to be the co-chair together with a Vietnamese counterpart. I was thrilled with this opportunity to serve in this capacity! With the backing of BGEA's staff and resources, and the numerous pastors and volunteers collaborating, the opportunity to impact all the churches citywide was exponentially greater than ever before. At the end, over 200 congregations in Hanoi and more than 550 congregations throughout North Vietnam had registered with the Festival office. The Love Hanoi Festival presented an ideal opportunity to cast the Love Hanoi vision to all the churches in Hanoi and North Vietnam and to demonstrate God's love in practical ways to citizens and city government alike. BGEA usually does include community services as part of the festival process, but not as central as it became in Hanoi.

LOVE HANOI = LOVE IN ACTION

The Love in Action team set the ambitious goal "to mobilize 100 churches and 500 volunteers to serve 5,000 hours per month to benefit their communities and Hanoi city." During the six months leading up to the Festival, Love in Action organized, sponsored, and inspired numerous community services with churches and partners. A total of 17 projects were listed. At least 3,600 people participated in the projects, ranging from blood drives to garbage cleanups to seminars to larger events.

Notably, the cleanup projects were organized in partnership with Keep Hanoi Clean, a non-Christian initiative in the CityPartners network. The cleanup project by Long Bien bridge was the largest project to date, with over 140 people clearing 14 tons of garbage from the under-serviced community. The local Hanoi TV news station covered it. Additionally, the drug rehab leaders organized a rally to reach the family and friends of the former addicts. It was the first time that the rehab leaders worked together to self-organize a joint event. At the end, over 50 people came forward in response to the testimonies and the gospel.

500 YEAR PROTESTANTISM ROUNDTABLE

The week before the Festival event, on December 3-4, 2017, a roundtable conference was organized by the Institute of Global Engagement (IGE) and hosted by Hanoi Bible College. "The goal of this Roundtable ... was to create a forum for academic discussion ... [and] to increase awareness about the history and development of the Evangelical faith in the world and

Vietnam," stated Hanoi Bible College. "In addition, the roundtable also considered objective data about the relationship between the evangelical faith and economics, politics, culture, society, and freedom, in order to find some positive directions for evangelicals to continue to develop into the future." As one of the 17 presenters, I had the privilege to present a paper entitled, *In Pursuit of Peace: Biblical Theology: How the doctrines of creation, fall, redemption, and new creation fuel Christian engagement in society.*[6]

One government scholar reflected, "This [event] turns out to be good. It gives us, government scholars, an opportunity to set foot into the church. From now on we will be less hesitant to come to church to attend events like this!" Because of the roundtable conference, the Institute of Religious Studies requested students of the Institute of Religious Studies to come to the Hanoi Evangelical Church and be taught by pastors about the gospel and how the gospel relates to various spheres of society, which eventually took place in March 2018. This is a remarkable step forward in building trust and mutual understanding.

LOVE IN ACTION SURVEY

On August 30, I presented the Love [Your City] seminar to about 45 church leaders. At the end, a survey was handed out to all participants to find out what community services the attendees were already doing. The initial results of the 31 respondents provided enough initial information to extend the survey citywide, and to cover the churches registered with the Festival office located in Hanoi Area 1 (a perimeter of one-hour travel from Hanoi).

During the following month of September 2017, volunteers surveyed by phone the 154 out of 214 church leaders in Hanoi Area 1 registered with the Love Hanoi Festival. The intent of the survey was to identify the current level of engagement of churches in community services. Basic data was gathered such as denomination, church name and address, and contact information. The participants then answered the same questions we used at the Love [Your City] seminar. The data was entered in Excel and initial conclusions were drawn from the information.

Reviewing these results, we decided to find out more about how churches organized the simplest and most popular projects (see Figure

7). These projects were blood drives, care for orphans, medical checkups, student scholarships, and soft skills training. Volunteers called the pastors who had implemented these projects and asked questions about the organizing process, the partner organizations, the participation of church members, the internal and external promotion activities, and any recommendations to other pastors who would like to organize the project. This information was noted and utilized for creating basic action steps to implementing the sample projects. After reviewing the data, I found two figures most promising to communicate publicly: 71% of the churches serve their communities and over 10,000 people had been helped by the churches during the previous year.

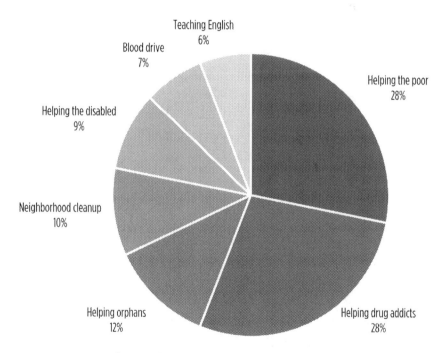

Figure 7: Projects by popularity

All this information was summarized and published in a Love in Action booklet. The first half contained two-page chapters outlining the vision for Love in Action, a brief description of Hanoi's context, a summary of the evangelical church history in Hanoi, a concise theology of city transformation, and concepts for collaboration and community services. The center spread provided the summary of the initial survey results. The second half of the booklet shared the vision for seed projects and outlined the sample projects that had been researched by the team. A total of 2,000 Vietnamese and 500 English booklets were printed and distributed to all the church leaders and many of their members to inspire them towards community engagement.

HANOI, JESUS LOVES YOU!

On December 8 and 9, the main Festival event took place. Only ten days prior to the event was the official permit extended, but only for the same Quang Ngua indoor stadium and not the National Stadium with 40,000 seating capacity. Two days prior to the event, permission was given to set up 3,000 stools outside. On the day of the event, the stadium manager told the organizers to add more stools. With two large LED screens outside, the seating capacity totaled 19,000.

A video report of the Love in Action activities was created to inspire more Christians to become more active and to inform government leaders about what we are doing. The video was shown twice during the Festival: first during the opening ceremony with government officials present, and again during the citywide worship celebration with almost all Hanoian Christians present. The government leaders were impressed by the church's contribution to society.

On Friday night, all the churches in Hanoi brought their friends to the Love Hanoi Festival. The music and performances were of high quality and the BGEA band had learned songs in Vietnamese. Franklin Graham gave a clear and concise presentation of the gospel, which was accurately translated into Vietnamese. At the end, over a thousand of more than 10,000 attendees came forward in response to the call to believe in Jesus. The message was clear—Jesus loves Hanoi!

On Saturday night, churches from all over North Vietnam came into the city in buses and flooded the stadium with the friends they had brought. Over 20,000 packed out the premises and thousands crowded towards the front in response to the gospel. After 20 years of plowing, sowing and watering in Hanoi, my wife and I were awestruck by the powerful love of God at work those two days. Over 4,250 people came forward in response to the good news. Praise God! Beyond imagination!

The second most memorable moment of the Festival took place during the worship celebration on Saturday morning. All pastors were called to step forward and formed a large circle in front of the stage, holding hands while singing a song on the unity in Christ based on John 17. Then the first Christian of the Hmong tribe was asked to pray for all these pastors. It was incredibly moving to see such unity among the evangelical leaders.

THE FESTIVAL MIGHT BE OVER BUT JESUS STILL LOVES HANOI!

After the Festival was over, in January 2018, the designer and manager of the Love Hanoi Festival website and Facebook page converted the Facebook page to the Love in Action page, thereby keeping the 1,000+ followers (1,385 likes as of August 5, 2018). The designer also created a new logo and a completely new website, taking the content of the Love in Action booklet and setting up both English and Vietnamese pages.[i] As a result, the content is no longer limited to the distribution of physical booklets but can reach Christians and non-Christians alike, impacting churches nationwide and around the world.

On April 14, the Festival's closing ceremony took place in HIF's facility. Having analyzed the Love in Action survey data, I had created and printed a professional looking report, and presented this to all the key church leaders and BGEA staff. It was impressive how much the evangelical community in Hanoi already contributes to their communities.

---

[i] Visit www.loveinaction.vn for more information.

CHAPTER 2

LOVE HANOI: THE CONTEXT

*Also, seek the peace and prosperity of the city to which
I have carried you into exile. Pray to the Lord for
it, because if it prospers, you too will prosper.*

Jeremiah 29:7

Having lived in Hanoi since 1997, it has been fascinating to witness the transformation the *Doi Moi* (renewal) policy has brought to the city. Most people in Hanoi have improved their lives as a direct result of *Doi Moi*. The orphans and foster children my wife and I helped in our first three years working at Friendship House now have their own families, homes, jobs and businesses. Although Hanoi's old quarter is still quaint and shows the influence from the Chinese and the French, the city is rapidly expanding and modernizing. Countless office towers and apartment buildings mushroom throughout the city. Traffic has changed from predominantly bicycles to mostly scooters and numerous cars, including SUVs, Mercedes, Bentleys, Rolls Royce, and a few luxury sports cars. Pricey smart phones are popular while fashion has become a priority. Students are sent overseas if the family can afford it.

With a history spanning over a thousand years and a population of almost ten million people, Hanoi's context is ancient, vast, and complex. Relatively speaking, the birth of the evangelical church here is a more recent phenomena, dating back just 100 years and, based on personal conversations, counting an estimated 7,000 evangelical Christians. At the reunification of Vietnam in 1975, it is said that only eight Christians were left in the Hanoi church. What has happened since, and particularly over the past five to ten years, is truly amazing considering the context.

Therefore, to understand the significance, it is important to learn about the context of Hanoi city and the local evangelical church. First, I will summarize the city's extensive history and describe the transformational impact of the *Doi Moi* policy. Second, I will give an overview of the Hanoi government and more specifically, the Committee of Religious Affairs and the new Law on Belief and Religion. Third, I will give a brief history of evangelicalism in Hanoi, describe the current situation of the church, and introduce Hanoi International Fellowship. The chapter concludes with an overview on how the Love Hanoi campaign is bringing transformation to the church and the city.

The History of Hanoi

On October 10, 2010 (popularized as 10/10/10), Hanoi celebrated its millennial anniversary. The grand celebration featured parades throughout the city and spectacular fireworks at night. Yet, before Hanoi became the capital, the area had already been inhabited for over a thousand years. People of the Viet tribe, migrating south from China, started populating the Red River Delta as early as the third century BC. It was not until AD 938 that the Viet threw off Chinese rule and became a tribute-paying state. Emulating the Chinese, Vietnam's kings called themselves emperors and exacted taxes from minority tribes.[7]

In the year 1010, Hanoi was chosen by Emperor Ly Thai To, the first ruler of the Ly dynasty (1009–1225), as the capital of Vietnam and called it Thang Long, meaning "Rising Dragon."[8] Several structures from this early period remain to this day, such as the Dong Co Temple, the One Pillar Pagoda (Dien Huu), the Bao Thien Tower by Hoan Kiem Lake, the Temple of Literature (Van Mieu), and the National University (Quoc Tu Giam). "Thus, only within a century did Thang Long become the largest and most important political, economic and cultural centre of the country."[9]

In 1802, the Nguyen dynasty moved the capital to the city of Hue. For some time, Thang Long was renamed to Dong King, which later "became corrupted by Europeans to Tonquin."[10] Upon the French colonial occupation in 1883, the whole region was referred to as Tonkin and the city was named *Ha Noi,* meaning "Between two rivers."[11] In 1902, Hanoi became the administrative capital of French Indochina.[12] During the Second World War, the Japanese occupied the country for five years between 1940-1945.[13]

For a brief time afterwards, the Viet Minh under Ho Chi Minh's leadership had control over the capital until the French reoccupation in 1946. It was not until the Dien Bien Phu victory in 1954 that the French ceased control of Hanoi and all northern Vietnam to Ho Chi Minh's army. During the years of what is referred to as the American War, Hanoi was bombed severely, resulting in significant damage. Surprisingly, many historic sites were spared and are still standing today. On April 30, 1975, the Northern Viet Cong took control of Saigon, and on July 2, 1976, the nation was reunited as the Socialist Republic of Vietnam with Hanoi as its capital.[14]

THE *DOI MOI* TRANSFORMATION

Due to the extreme post-war poverty, at the sixth congress of the Vietnam Communist Party in December 1986, a new policy called *Doi Moi* was adopted. The term *đổi mới* means new (*mới*) change (*đổi*) and has often been translated as reform, renewal, or renovation. "Most of the population still lived in poverty in 1986, the majority far worse off than at [the 1975] Reunification."[15] Hanoi's economy, however, became stagnant until the restructuring in 1991 to "industry, trade, tourism, services and agriculture."[16] Since then, the capital has seen rapid development with the aid of foreign direct investments from friendly nations, international corporations, non-governmental organizations (NGOs), and global institutions such as the World Bank, the International Monetary Fund, and the Asian Development Bank.

The *Doi Moi* reformation truly brought transformation to the nation, lifting millions of citizens out of poverty. "The $1.90-a-day poverty rate fell from 50 percent in the early 1990s to 3 percent today. Using the General Statistics Office-World Bank standard, poverty incidence fell from about 58 percent to 13.5 percent over the same period."[17] Steve Price-Thomas, Advocacy and Campaigns Director at Oxfam International, calculated that between 1993 and 2006, "an average rate of 5,736 people [were] moving over the poverty line each day."[18]

In *Vietnam 2035: Toward Prosperity, Creativity, Equity, and Democracy,* the World Bank and the Ministry of Planning and Investment of Vietnam report,

> Renovations in development thinking introduced under Đổi Mới enabled four key transitions: from centrally-planned and subsidized resource allocation to more market-based allocation; from a predominantly state-owned economy to a multi-actor economy with an increasingly dynamic private sector; from a closed economy to an increasingly open and internationally integrated economy; and from centralized to decentralized governance structures. Vietnam is aiming for a new development dynamism toward "prosperity, creativity, equity, and democracy" by 2035. It is moving toward realizing national aspirations for "a prosperous people, and a strong, democratic, equitable, and civilized country, in which all people enjoy an abundant, free, and happy life and are given conditions for their comprehensive development," as defined in the country's Constitution and in the "Credo for Country's Development in the Transition Period" of the Communist Party of Vietnam (CPV).[19]

HANOI GOVERNMENT

Vietnam is divided into four levels of government administration: national, provincial, district, and municipality (see Figure 8). Twenty percent of the municipalities are classified as urban. These urban cities are categorized into six classes, of which only two cities qualify for the top "Special Class" level, namely Hanoi and Ho Chi Minh City. These two, along with Hai Phong, Da Nang, and Can Tho, are also considered provincial cities, directly managed under Vietnam's central government. The higher the status, the greater the autonomy from provincial authority. Hanoi, therefore, is a special class province city divided into districts and wards. Financially speaking, however, the city's "budget is simply part of the state budget and, in principle, only serves to implement at the local level the plan defined at the national level."[20]

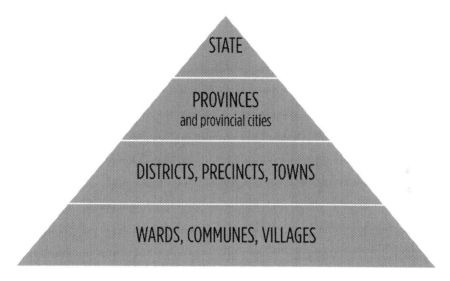

Figure 8. The four levels of Sub-National Government of the Vietnamese State[21]

In Hanoi, a province city, the various government departments report both up to their national ministries and horizontal at the provincial level. The Hanoi People's Committee provides oversight over 17 departments, 15 offices, boards, and committees, 12 urban districts, 17 rural districts, one town, and 11 subordinate units. Former director of the Hanoi Police Department, Major General Nguyen Duc Chung, was appointed chairman of Hanoi's People's Committee at the end of 2015.

Although the chairman of the People's Committee is considered to be the mayor of the city, it is the "Party Committee [that] is the leading organ of the Communist Party of Vietnam of each of the country's cities."[22] Two months after Mayor Chung's appointment, Deputy Prime Minister Hoang Trung Hai was appointed as the Secretary of the Hanoi Party Committee. The party's secretary gives the directives to and approves the plans of the mayor's office. At the same time, the Fatherland Front continues to have significant influence in the politics of the city.

Starting in 2013, church leaders in Hanoi have built good relationships with Hanoi's mayor. When at the end of 2015 Mr. Chung was appointed mayor of Hanoi, we church leaders already had a good relationship with the Major General. At the following Tet holiday (Vietnamese New Year) in 2016, a delegation of pastors representing the evangelical community of Hanoi, including myself, went to visit Mayor Chung at the city hall. We had the opportunity to speak a blessing over him in his new office as mayor, along with other city leaders present. Later that year, Mayor Chung gave the permission to celebrate the 100-year anniversary of the Hanoi Evangelical Church in the Quang Ngua stadium. Over 6,000 Christians attended this worshipful event, a first in Hanoi's history.

When the leading pastors of Hanoi proposed the idea of organizing another festival to celebrate the 500-year anniversary of the Reformation in 2017, the mayor was quick to give verbal approval for the use of the National Stadium, which has a seating capacity over 40,000. Yet, when it came to obtain the permit, Mr. Hai of Hanoi's Party Committee was able to override Mayor Chung's decision and deny the request. The festival was eventually held at the smaller Quang Ngua stadium, with the permit granted only ten days prior to the event. This example illustrates the decision-making power of the Communist Party over the People's Committee.

GOVERNMENT COMMITTEE FOR RELIGIOUS AFFAIRS

Established in 1955, "the Government Committee for Religious Affairs is an agency under the Ministry of Home Affairs, which functions as an advisory body to assist the Minister of Home Affairs in the state management of religious affairs throughout the country and to provide services." Since 2007, the Government Committee for Religious Affairs (GCRA) has been organized under the Ministry of Home Affairs, with each provincial office of the GCRA placed under the provincial department of Home Affairs. "At this time, 64 provinces and cities nationwide have 38 religious committees, 11 ethnic minority religions committees, ten ethnic minority committees and one religious office belonging to the provincial People's Committee Office (Lang Son), four Ethnic Minorities Committees (with religious observers) such as Son La,

Lai Chau, Dien Bien and Lao Cai," accounting for "699 full time officers." At the city level, the Hanoi Department of Religious Affairs was placed under Hanoi's Department of Home Affairs in 2010.[23]

The GCRA is organized in the following 15 departments :

1. Catholic Department
2. Buddhist Department
3. Protestant Department
4. Cao Dai Department
5. Department of Other Religions
6. Department of International Relations
7. Legal Department - Inspection
8. Department of Organization and Personnel
9. Office
10. Southern Religious Affairs Department
11. Religion Policy Research Institute
12. Journal of Religious Affairs
13. Information Center
14. School of Religious Work
15. Religion Publishing House[24]

The chairman of the GCRA is Dr. Vu Chien Thang who is supported by three Deputy Chiefs. The Hanoi Department of Religious Affairs (HDRA) is directed by Mr. Phạm Tien Dung. Missionary visas for HIF's staff are approved by GCRA, National Security Police, Hanoi City Police, and Hanoi People's Committee. HDRA processed the registration of Hanoi International Fellowship and HIF's public events, which were approved at all the higher levels. Besides GCRA and its Hanoi department, the Ministry of Security Police and the Ministry of Foreign Affairs both have a religious affairs department with a Protestant office at the national and city level.

To build and maintain relationships, each year on the occasion of Tet, I join other lead pastors in Hanoi to visit GCRA, HDRA, City Police, and other district offices. More recently, some government offices have reciprocated the friendly exchange by visiting our offices during the

Christmas season. These are promising signs of a growing friendly posture between church and state.

LAW ON BELIEF AND RELIGION

Vietnam is one of few countries in the world with a religious law. On January 1, 2018, the new Law on Belief and Religion (02/2016/QH14) went into effect. This law replaced the previous Ordinance on Belief and Religion, and the Decree (92/2012/ND-CP) implementation guidelines. Article 1.1 of the new law states, "This Law provides for the right to freedom of belief and religion; belief activities and religious activities; religious organizations; rights and obligations of agencies, organizations and individuals relating to belief activities and religious activities."[25]

The law defines *belief* as "a person's faith which is expressed through rites associated with traditional customs and habits in order to bring spiritual peacefulness to individuals and communities," and *religion* as "a person's faith existing together with a system of concepts and activities, including subject for worshipping, dogmas, canon laws, rites and organization."[26] The law differentiates between religious practice, religious activities, and religious organizations, the first being an "expression of religious faith," the second "dissemination of religion," and the third "a grouping of believers."[27] This differentiation is important as it determines the three levels of registration.

Article 6.1 of the Law on Belief and Religion states that "Every person has the right to freedom of belief and religion and freedom to follow or not to follow a belief or religion."[28] Religious activities, festivals, gatherings, and organizations must be registered with the relevant People's Committee at the Ward, District or Provincial level. A religious organization can only receive registration after it has operated certified religious activities for at least five years (Article 21.1).[29] Registration of religious organizations will be decided by the provincial level People's Committee and issued by the provincial Department for Religious Affairs (Article 22.3).[30] Ordinations must be reported within 20 days to Religious Affairs, which may request the religious organization to revoke the ordination if the person in question is not law abiding (Article 33).[31] Functionaries (heads and board members of religious organizations operating in multiple provinces and heads of training institutions), however, must receive prior approval from the government before the appointment takes place and before the functionary is transferred to another province. In addition, religious training institutions can now be registered following the procedures outlined in Articles 37-42.[32]

Of particular interest is Chapter VI on "Religious Activities; Publishing, Education, Health, Social Assistance, Charitable and Humanitarian Activities of Religious Organizations."[33] Section 2 spells out the laws of foreign-related religious activities. Article 47 allows foreigners to register religious gatherings with the province-level People's Committee.[34] This registration process can be done directly with the provincial Department of Religious Affairs without needing to register under a Vietnamese religious organization, as was the case for HIF when we first registered under the Evangelical Church of Vietnam-North in 2017. In early 2018, two Korean churches in Hanoi immediately registered. HIF received its independent registration in 2019, the first international church in Vietnam to receive this status.

International congregations can use any legal premise and are no longer limited to meet in religious facilities (like church buildings). It must be noted, however, that foreign groups cannot register as a religious organization, thus only receive permission for organizing their religious activities at the stated premises. The registration document provides them with a non-commercial license, which can be used to sign contracts and obtain visas for pastoral staff.

Additional articles state that foreign religious organizations may operate and ordain within Vietnam. Foreigners may enroll at religious training institutions in Vietnam, and religious organizations in Vietnam may join foreign religious organizations, but all upon request and prior approval from the government. Yet, it must be kept in mind that, according to Article 46, "preaching outside religious establishment or lawful premises" still requires permission from the district or provincial level of government.[35]

Section 3 under Chapter VI contains only two articles, each with one sentence. Article 54 states, "Entitled to publishing religious texts, books and other publications related to belief and religion; producing, exporting and importing cultural products related to belief and religion and religious articles in accordance with publication laws and other relevant laws." Article 55 states that religious organizations are "[e]ntitled to engaging in education, training, health, social assistance, charitable and humanitarian activities in accordance with relevant laws."[36] Churches and denominations should, in theory, be allowed to register schools, clinics, hospitals, and non-profit organizations. It is now up to Christian leaders to explore the new opportunities and probe where the boundaries are.

HISTORY OF EVANGELICALISM IN HANOI

In 2016, the Hanoi Evangelical Church (HEC)[j] celebrated its centennial anniversary. This celebration was a significant milestone, considering that what the church has lived through in those hundred years. The church was founded in 1916 during the French colonial occupation, survived the Japanese WWII subjugation, and lived through the prolonged battle for control over Hanoi between the Viet Minh and the French.[37] When the nation was split between North and South at the Geneva Accord in 1954, "hundreds of thousands, mainly Catholics and Protestants, went South."[38] This exodus left a small remnant of evangelical Christians in Hanoi. One "generous estimate" has only 6,000 Protestant Christians located in North Vietnam in 1973 compared to 160,000 Protestant Christians nationwide.[39]

The Evangelical Church of Vietnam (ECVN) was established in 1911 in Danang (then called Tourane) by missionaries and converts of the Christian & Missionary Alliance (C&MA). They had inherited the work of the British and Foreign Bible Society, as the BFBS missionary named Bonnet wanted to relocate to Hanoi.[40] By 1916, the C&MA sent missionaries to Hanoi in the north and later to Saigon in the south by 1918.[41]

William Cadman and Grace Hazenburg-Cadman, who had met in Vietnam, became the first C&MA missionary couple to station in Hanoi.

---

[j] See www.hoithanhhanoi.com for more information.

In their first published correspondence dated November 11, 1916, Grace provides a picturesque description of the city at that time:

> Here are the constant ebb and flow of the sea of humanity: tens of thousands of men, women, and children, active and eager in their pursuit of pleasure, or in their daily labor. The buzzing of the electric street-cars, the rumble of trains, the whir of the automobiles as they rush past our house, all remind us that we are a part of the big modern world, even though we are in the heart of heathen Annam, or rather Indo-China.[42]

Hanoi in 1916 counted "135,000 souls—this teeming population closely packed in the miles on miles of houses." By 1917, the Cadmans held their first baptism, and by 1921 their little congregation was made up of 17 converts.[43] Grace had graduated with an MBA and studied Greek and Hebrew, while William was a printer by trade. This combination of skills proved to be perfect for translating and publishing the first Protestant Vietnamese Bible, which came off the press within a ten-year timespan—an amazing accomplishment. With the press purchased in 1920, five million pages of Christian literature were produced per year. William and Grace served until the end and were both buried in Vietnam.[44]

It was not until 1929 that other Protestant denominations found their way to Vietnam, namely the Seventh Day Adventists who "directed much of their proselytizing at ECVN followers."[45] Much later, Mennonite Central Committee (1954), World Evangelization Crusade (1956), Southern Baptists (1959), and Assemblies of God (1972) missionaries arrived.[46] Since all these dates are post-1954 and pre-1975, it can be safely assumed that none but the C&MA had planted a church in Hanoi.

The C&MA, and likely also most these other denominations, were primarily concerned with saving souls. As Grace Cadman wrote in her 1916 article, "with God's blessing souls can be saved."[47] This quote provides insight into the question why the dichotomy between sacred and secular is so strong among the evangelical churches in Vietnam. It was the Mennonites who paved the way for non-traditional mission work, such as charities, healthcare, and education. During the war period, World Vision,

World Relief, and other Christian organizations came to provide care for the wounded and relief for the nation.[48]

In more recent years, during the 1990s and early 2000s, only seven out of 70 active denominations were registered in the South, predominately those denominations that had existed before 1975.[49] Other denominations were established as informal house church networks, primarily in Ho Chi Minh City, with branches in Hanoi.[50] Some were splits from the ultra-conservative ECVN-South after irreconcilable disagreements over the charismatic gifts of the Holy Spirit.[51] Some groups splintered due to interpersonal conflict between leaders or the lure of funding from foreign denominations.[52] In Hanoi, a few unique denominations were established by Vietnamese who had returned from overseas countries such as Hong Kong, Germany, and Russia. For a long time, these leaders and groups were suspicious of each other. "In 2009," reports Reimer, "a number of house churches in Hanoi and other parts of the north formed the Hanoi Christian Fellowship."[53] Through the work of the Holy Spirit, a strong sense of unity and collaboration is experienced among the evangelical churches in the city and nationwide.

HANOI INTERNATIONAL FELLOWSHIP

Soon after the *Doi Moi*, foreigners made their way to Hanoi, including a small number of Christians. In solidarity, they gathered on Sundays for worship and fellowship in their homes. These included Catholics, Seventh Day Adventists, Nazarenes, Mennonites, Lutherans, and Evangelicals. In 1995, a group of evangelical expats felt the need for a more contemporary style of worship services and Bible-based sermons. In August that year, they met in the living room of Stewart Stemple. Although Stemple had requested permission from the government, he had not received a formal reply. By November, a steering committee was formed, and a statement of faith was adopted from the Evangelical Church of Bangkok. Despite not having received official permission from the government, the international church called Hanoi International Fellowship (HIF) was born.

When our family first arrived in Hanoi in 1997, HIF consisted of about 40 people meeting in a small hotel. I joined the steering committee in 1998 and frequently served as a worship leader. In 2005, when the church had around 150 people in attendance, I was asked to become HIF's pastor. Earlier that year, the church had gone through an identity crisis, realizing that for its first decade HIF had been primarily inward focused. The leadership experienced God's call for HIF to become outward focused in reaching fellow expatriates and serving the city.

I attended the conference of the Missional International Church Network (MICN) in the UAE to learn more about how HIF could become externally focused in our given context. As I've said in the Introduction, it was at MICN that I personally experienced a new paradigm shift to think missionally about HIF's vision and practice. It is this missional journey that has brought me and HIF to the posture of seeking the peace and prosperity of the city in collaboration with the citywide church and city government. Over the years, it has become so evident that our peace and prosperity is directly related and dependent on the peace and prosperity of the city (Jeremiah 29:7).

Loving Hanoi Together

Church leaders in Hanoi are optimistic about the growth of their congregations. Many are thinking about future church buildings, and some have bought properties on the lower-cost outskirts of the city. With the growing unity and collaboration among church leaders, a kingdom movement has already begun to bring about urban transformation. The drug rehab ministries by various house churches have given tangible evidence of the power of the gospel to transform the lives of former addicts and prostitutes. One of these ministries has been given open doors at government rehabs to minister freely and has recently obtained 5,000 square meters of land to build a large rehab center. Today there are six networks with 24 centers in Hanoi rehabilitating over 600 former addicts, supported by many other churches locally and globally.

On December 29, 2015, the Institute of Religious Studies and ECVN-North organized the first academic conference entitled, "Social Responsibility of Evangelicals in the Past and Present." The 12 presented papers were compiled into a book form, a first ever in the history of the evangelical church. Although foreigners were not allowed this time, it prepared the way to organize the next conference with international participation. That roundtable conference, as mentioned previously, eventually took place the week before the festival with foreign delegates from World Evangelical Alliance, Baylor University, the German Government, Hanoi Bible College, and HIF.

With the increasing openness of the government towards the participation of the evangelical community in society, it is the right time to explore the opportunities the new Law on Belief and Religion provides, particularly in the social, health, and education sectors. Lord willing, within a few years the evangelical community in Hanoi will see the founding of many Christian non-profits, clinics, and schools. The Love Hanoi campaign helps to keep our focus external, to love the city and her citizens unconditionally, and to collaborate across various boundaries for the peace and prosperity of Hanoi. It is during the seven-year journey and my doctoral studies that I have discovered and developed the five steps to start citywide movements, which I will introduce in the next chapter.

CHAPTER 3

LOVE HANOI: THE STEPS

Then I said to them, "You see the trouble we are in: Jerusalem lies in ruins, and its gates have been burned with fire. Come, let us rebuild the wall of Jerusalem, and we will no longer be in disgrace." I also told them about the gracious hand of my God on me and what the king had said to me. They replied, "Let us start rebuilding." So they began this good work.

Nehemiah 2:17-18

Nehemiah and the citizens of Jerusalem rebuilt the city walls within 54 days! Rebuilding society took Nehemiah the rest of his working career, with great persecution and aggravation, but also with great exhilaration and celebration. The project did not launch overnight, although you might get that idea when reading the abbreviated introduction. The organization of people did not go without its challenges (the nobles refused to join the effort and worked counterproductively). The sustainability apparently had failed, which Nehemiah discovered after he had returned from a few years' break. The Love Jerusalem campaign, if I may call it that, was a process with many steps and stages. So will your Love [Your City] initiative if you were to start one.

Based on my experience from the Love Hanoi campaign, my research for my doctoral degree, and my Love [Your City] seminar which I have presented in various countries, I have developed the five steps to start citywide movements (see Figure 9). These steps will take you on a journey from beliefs to habits to practice to collaboration to transformation. In this chapter I will briefly introduce each step so that you will have the big picture before zooming in to each one.

35

Figure 9: 5 steps of citywide movements

STEP 1: PRINCIPLES

The first step towards citywide movements is to lay the foundation for biblical principles upon which you can build an extensive relational ministry across all sorts of boundaries. The Love [Your City] model is not just some new idea, a new trend that will soon pass, or a method from a secular source. From before Eden, God intended for cities to exist. After all, He is named the "architect and builder" of the heavenly "city with foundations" for which we are waiting (Hebrews 11:10; Revelation 21:2). These foundations we need today to answer Jesus' model prayer, "Your name [be glorified], Your kingdom come, Your will be done, [in our city] as it is in heaven" (Matthew 6:9-10). Since the days of creation, humanity has been mandated to fill the earth and steward creation. How can Christians be biblical placemakers? What does it mean to "[s]eek the shalom of the city"? If God's kingdom were to come to our city, what would that look like? A well-rounded theology of the city, shalom, placemaking, and the kingdom of God will help you ensure you are building on a good foundation of biblical principles.

STEP 2: POSTURE

People learn more about us from our non-verbal cues than from our words. The way we posture ourselves when speaking with someone tells them what we really think and believe. Sadly, the posture of Christians towards one another and the city has not always been positive (that is an understatement). Pastors and church leaders tend to think church-centric as church life is demanding work. Churches can also retreat into an escapism of thinking, see themselves as outsiders to society and the city, and become defensive or aggressive towards the public (and even other churches). To launch or be part of a citywide movement, church leaders and members need to shift their posture to a more integrated stance towards the city, their immediate community, and the poor. A transformed mind, resulting from the biblical principles and the Spirit's work, will help you to "have the same mindset as Christ Jesus" in relationships with others (Philippians 2:5).

STEP 3: PROCESS

Once you and your church or organization decide to seek the peace of the city and get involved in the community, where do you start the actual work? Over recent years, new concepts have been developed that will help you think through the process of doing projects. The Missional Cycle explains why starting conversations about beliefs is like starting backwards. Serving with the people you want to reach to meet their felt needs leads to building trust and increasing conversations at the social, intellectual, and spiritual levels. Christian Community Development (CCD) builds on this cycle to present a process of eight phases, which helps churches and groups to think and plan. It is important to work *with* the people and as much as possible to use *their* resources. The Asset Based Community Development (ABCD) model, which was developed by Christian community development practitioners, emphasizes this approach and will turn your church literally inside-out. Seed Projects are a great way to start engaging your community and I have listed small and short-term project ideas for quick wins in your citywide movement.

STEP 4: PARTNER

What is partnership and how is it different from networking? What does a citywide ministry network look like? How can you collaborate across the sectors of society and partner across boundaries? What do you need to pay attention to when partnering cross-culturally and working with a culturally diverse team? This chapter is the nuts and bolts section of the book. A favorite topic of mine, you will find a variety of concepts, models, and diagrams. Partnership is the crux of citywide movements and getting this right is critical for the Love [Your City] campaign's success. The movement's partnership and catalytic team will make or break the momentum.

STEP 5: PEOPLE

At the end, the citywide movement is all about people. Knowing the leader's function and skills needed for each stage of the movement will help to recognize the right person for the right job at the right time. Eight perspectives of transformational leadership will guide the movement's leaders to stay biblically grounded and reflective of Jesus' leadership paradigm. A variety of methods to gather people are described, from small groups on a bus tour to one-day citywide conferences to three-day large group consultations. It can get exciting once you start bringing larger groups of people together for inspiration and collaboration to implement your Love [Your City] campaign. This chapter will help you in gathering and leading them.

Ready? Set? Let's go to Step 1: Principles.

PART TWO:

5 STEPS TO CITYWIDE MOVEMENTS

CHAPTER 4

PRINCIPLES

*For he [Abraham] was looking forward to the city with
foundations, whose architect and builder is God.*

Hebrews 11:10

Little did I know how much my life would change when my Lutheran
missionary friend gave me Ray Bakke's book, *A Theology as Big as the City*.
In it, Ray journeys through Scripture from Genesis to Revelation, revealing
how much the Bible speaks about cities. With personal anecdotes from
his 30+ years of pastoral experience in inner-city Chicago, it was easy to
connect to the reinterpreted ancient urban stories. As the Senior Associate
for Large Cities with the Lausanne Committee for World Evangelization,
Ray visited over 200 cities between 1979 and 1995 before writing this
book.

As I drove my scooter through the busy city streets, I started to look
at Hanoi differently. It dawned on me that in the ten years of ministry
in the city, I had never looked at Hanoi from a theological perspective; I
had never considered what the Bible has to say about the whole city. Sure,
I had a theology for missions, for church, for social work, for worship,
and even for marketplace ministry, but not for the WHOLE city. Over
time, I came to realize that, to my embarrassment, I was a consumer of
the city, not a contributor. I used the city for my ministry agenda but had
not considered how I might serve for the benefit of the city. This was a
significant paradigm shift for me.

The first step to city transformation is the transformation of our own
beliefs in what the Bible says about cities. Although the biblical narrative
starts in a garden, it ends in a city. God is not trying to undo the fall of

humanity by working backwards to Eden but moving forwards to the New Jerusalem.

This chapter will introduce foundational **biblical principles** needed to start citywide movements. First, a theology *of* and *for* the city is presented. Then, a much broader topic is discussed, namely a theology of place. Third, we zoom out further to unwrap the meaning of the Hebrew concept of shalom. Lastly, a theology of the kingdom will set us up for the following chapters, allowing us to collaborate across boundaries to seek the shalom of the city in which God has placed us.

A THEOLOGY OF THE CITY

At the end of our visit in 2016 with the newly-appointed Hanoi Chief of Police, as we (a delegation of city pastors) were standing and shaking hands ready to go, the chief invited us to present at the upcoming conference on the topic of urban environment. Major General Doan Duy Khuong asked if we could share what the Bible teaches on caring for the environment. *But this is not what seminaries teach pastors in theology class (though they should).* A quick online search offered few resources. Pastor Paul Bui of Hanoi Evangelical Church put a paper together and made a presentation at the citywide conference. The city government had even printed a large vertical banner with a Scripture verse on it, besides Buddhist and government slogans.

This was not the first time Pastor Paul was asked to present a theology paper at a citywide consortium. Previously he had been invited to give a biblical perspective on the topic of genetic manipulation. Hanoi's government is interested to learn the various religious perspectives on the difficult issues they are facing. Are we as pastors ready for this? For decades we desired improved relationships between state and government. Now we must not be "of those who shrink back ... but of those who have faith" (Hebrews 10:38-39).

Ray Bakke was right when he said, "For me the Bible has to confront the why questions and all the issues of urban life." It is not enough to do a study on the word *city* in the Bible and develop a theology *of* the city. Christians and practitioners must have a theology *for* the city, for all the issues they will face in the urban context. It must be "a *theology as big as the city*," as Bakke's book is appropriately titled. This theology must answer questions such as the following:

- How shall I read the world?
- Why did my baby die? (I know how, but why?)
- Where can I find an environmental theology to confront a toxic planet?
- How shall we reflect on the ever-widening gap between the "have" and the "have-nots"?
- What is the relationship between the Christian faith and other faiths?
- What do we do about the increasingly prevalent issue of sexual identity?
- What texts, themes or stories address these and other issues?[54]

The Bible is filled with urban stories that we in the 21st century can connect to. Most of the Scriptures was written in the urban context primarily for city dwellers. Moses wrote his works as the "mayor" of a "mobile city" of an estimated two million Israelites and migrant refugees. Most of the historic and prophetic books were written in and for Israel's capital city. Many of the Psalms were penned in Jerusalem, sang on the way to urban festivals, even exalting the city of God. Consider the Gospels, where Jesus journeyed from city to town to village. The Book of Acts and the Epistles showcase God's global urban mission strategy, with the Apostle Paul planting churches in strategic city centers of the Roman Empire. The grand finale, of course, takes place in the fantastic and gigantic New Jerusalem.

The following are but a few examples of **Scriptural principles** for the urban context drawn out of biblical narratives.

Genesis is not only the first book of the Bible, but also a Greek translation of the book's first Hebrew word, *bereshith*, meaning "in the beginning." The opening chapter of Genesis gives an account of creation's origins resulting from God's will and spoken word. "In the beginning God created the heavens and the earth" (Genesis 1:1) is a summary of all that follows: the creation of light to separate darkness, of sky to separate the waters above and below, and of land to separate the sea. As order was brought to the physical chaos, God brought forth living vegetation and creatures to fill the sky, land and sea just formed. Each step of the way, God looked at His work and was satisfied, like an artist would with his painting or a musician with her song.

Then, on the sixth day, God made His masterpiece, His *magnum opus*, creating humanity from the dust and breathing it to life with His Spirit. Both male and female were made into the likeness of the Trinity, image bearers of God, vice-regents and ambassadors upon planet earth. With free will and faith, they enjoyed a perfect relationship with their creator, surrounding creation, and each other. It was so good that God took a day's rest to thoroughly enjoy the work of His hands.

Yet, not all was complete, and more work was to be done. Starting with a small patch of fertile and resource-rich land, watered by four winding rivers, the garden of Eden was to be extended until humanity would fill the whole earth. This work was to be a collaborative effort between God and people, like a parent would raise a child, teach their trade, and join into business together. As humanity would multiply, the wild world would be cultivated and managed, maintaining the harmonious relationship between creator and creation.

It is tempting to presume that the pristine image of the garden in Eden was the only plan God had in mind when placing humankind on earth; that the only outcome after filling and subduing the wild planet would be a scattering of gardens; and that Christians today should turn society back from city building to garden making. After all, did cities not appear until after the fall? Were cities not the result of humanity's attempt at independence from God? Are cities not the creation of humankind and the center of evil? In the early 18th century, US President Thomas Jefferson said, "I view great American cities as pestilential to the morals, health, and the liberties of man."[55] Man's power is first of all the result of hardening his heart against God: man affirms that he is strong, conquers the world, and builds cities."[56]

Although the biblical narrative starts in a garden, it ends in a city! Genesis 1-2 and Revelation 21-22 form the bookends of the Bible and clearly demonstrate the progression from garden to city, both created by God, the builder and architect (Hebrews 11:10). The size of God's city is so phenomenal that it can only be interpreted as metaphorical. At almost five million square kilometers in footprint and 2,225 kilometers high, it is half the size of the USA and 250 times as high as Mount Everest! Based on calculations of the potential population of the Shimizu Mega-City Pyramid, the New Jerusalem would be able to house 1.8 trillion people! Scientists estimate that 105 billion people have lived on planet earth so far.[57] The New Jerusalem clearly sends a message: There is plenty of room for everyone!

The point is this: God had always intended for cities to be built and to exist. The narrative of Scripture does not move backwards to the garden, but forwards to the city. The seeds of the city were sown in the garden of Eden with the mandate to multiply and fill the earth, and to subdue and govern all creation. The gathering of people into communities and the expansion of communities into cities is inevitable as humanity would spread out and steward their collective responsibilities.

First and foremost, cities would have been centers of worship if all people were to have stayed in right relationship with God. Cities would have been righteous, which would have permeated all of society and technology. Cities would have been centers of culture, creativity, invention, education, economy, and governance, very much like they are today but without crime and evil. It is hard for us to imagine such cities today, but clearly this is what God had (and still has) in mind. Throughout Scripture, we can find glimpses of God's vision and design for cities, particularly for the prototype city of Jerusalem, and the futuristic projections of the New Jerusalem.

What then is this vision of a godly city? How then can we go about designing cities with that vision in mind? What could be done to contribute to our cities today? How can we work together towards the transformation of cities to see God's kingdom come and His will be done in our cities as it is in the heavenly archetype? What we need is a theology of placemaking, because the story between the bookends, from Eden's garden to the New Jerusalem, is the story of placemaking.

A THEOLOGY OF PLACEMAKING

It was a mispronunciation that I'll never be able to live down (at least not with my family) because it was quite funny. It proves that I am still an ESL (English as a Second Language) speaker. During my sermon series *God of the City*, I was quite excited to make this pun the main point. On paper it looked great! The pun was this: "The *awr* went awry!" But instead of pronouncing awry like it should be, "uh-wry," I said, "awe-rie." Well, the native English speakers had fun, but at least it is a pun I'll never forget!

The Hebrew word for city is *awr*, which can refer to an enclosed space, a town, or a city like Jerusalem, the City of David. The first "city" in the Bible is the one Cain built and named after his son Enoch (Genesis 4:17). Most likely, Cain had created a fence or wall around a compound of living structures. His parents had been exiled from Eden's garden and Cain, after murdering his brother Abel, had been expelled further yet into the wilderness. Once his wife started having children, Cain needed to protect his family from others who might want to harm them—as he had done to his own brother. Not a great start for the reputation of cities in Scripture, a walled in place to protect families from murder! Sin has a way to taint every good thing.

Walls were what defined cities throughout ages past, to keep the good people in and the bad ones out. In Hanoi, the ancient city wall's gates to the North, East, West and South can still be found today. In Holland, concentric circles of walls and canals can be found in historic cities, which were constructed as the cities expanded.

In the Old Testament, the next mention of cities is found in conjunction with the name Nimrod, a great-grandson of Noah. Not only was he a mighty warrior (which leaves the question, "Who was he fighting with and why?"), but also a builder of cities and kingdoms. His claim to fame is listed in Genesis 10:10-12,

The first centers of his kingdom were Babylon, Uruk, Akkad and Kalneh, in Shinar. From that land he went to Assyria, where he built Nineveh, Rehoboth Ir, Calah and Resen, which is between Nineveh and Calah—which is the great city.

Noah's descendants dispersed across land and sea, filling the earth and subduing it. That Nimrod laid the foundations of cities famous and infamous throughout the following eras of the Old Testament is profound. That he did so while fighting his cousins, to protect his people from attack, and to later become cities of dread and terror, leaves much to be desired.

The *awr* really goes awry (here's the pun!) in the chapter that follows. Within just eight verses, the reputation of cities is so badly damaged that Christians today still doubt God's intent. Having mastered the skill of brick making, the people in Shinar said, "Come, let us build ourselves a city, with a tower that reaches to the heavens, so that we may make a name for ourselves; otherwise we will be scattered over the face of the whole earth" (Genesis 11:4). Yet, what seemed so significant to the builders, compared to God's greatness, it was so tiny that He had to come down in order "to see the city and the tower" (v. 5).

Defiantly, humanity had directly opposed God's mandate to fill the earth, building a tower as if they could somehow reach God on their own merit, intent to make their own name great instead of the Lord's. God would have nothing of it, and as if with a flick of a magician's hand, He confused their language, stopped the building project, and dispersed the people across the planet. It is no wonder that tribal cultures and ancient languages today still maintain the same or similar biblical stories from before the Babel experience, as they share a common history.[k]

The *awr* had indeed gone awry (I love saying this!), but this does not prove that cities are innately evil. The making of places, after all, was God's idea and His first act after breathing life into His human creation. The creator had made an image of Himself in bodily form and now needed somewhere to put him down, to house him, to feed him, and to enjoy his company. Therefore, He "planted a garden in the east, in Eden" so that He could "put the man he had formed" and together continue the creation project (Genesis 2:8). God had made a place for man and woman to live and to dwell with Him, to love and to procreate, to work and to launch a

---

[k]   Chinese characters, for example, contain several Genesis stories. For more details, visit www.answersingenesis.org/genesis/chinese-characters-and-genesis

management project that would cover the rest of planet earth. God was the first homemaker, an honorable and glorifying profession!

Picture in your mind the pristine garden, which had its boundaries within the larger and fruitful Eden, which was surrounded by a wild planet yet to subdue, amid the solar system and stars. Now translate this into the language of the tabernacle and temple: Think of the garden as the Holy of Holies, a private and intimate space as part of the Holy Place, a built and protected structure within the larger outer court, which is walled in from the surrounding world. The garden was the original Holy of Holies, the most holy place where God dwells with humanity! God's intent for placemaking had always been to extend the boundaries of the garden, the most holy place, until it would extend across the world and all people would dwell within it and with His presence.

Now project the garden and the Holy of Holies to the eternal New Jerusalem. The cubicle space within the tabernacle structure called the Holy of Holies now has become a massive cube of a city on astronomical scale which could house a hundred times over the 100+ billion people who ever lived! And the garden is still there!

> *Then the angel showed me the river of the water of life, bright as crystal, flowing from the throne of God and of the Lamb through the middle of the street of the city; also, on either side of the river, the tree of life with its twelve kinds of fruit, yielding its fruit each month. The leaves of the tree were for the healing of the nations.* (Revelation 22:1-2)

Placemaking and city-building have always been God's Plan A, creating sacred spaces where He and humanity would dwell together. It is no wonder that the tabernacle was modeled after a heavenly pattern which God had shown Moses on Mount Sinai. It is an idealistic picture of perfect harmony between God, humanity, and creation; an idealism that once was and one time will be true. It is an image of perfect peace, or what the Bible describes as *shalom*. Continuing our journey through Scripture, it is Melchizedek's story that paints the first picture of the City of Shalom.

A Theology of *Shalom*

I was astounded, felt betrayed, and grieved deeply. A close friend of mine
had fallen and I had not seen it coming. Craig and his wife Sally (not their
real names) had been married for 25 years and missionaries for 20. We had
lived close to each other when they arrived in Hanoi and had children of
similar ages. We had fun together, worshiped together, and strategized
together. Craig and I had served together on the church board, traveled
together, and launched a new ministry together. Until one day, after
returning from a trip to Thailand, Craig did not return home, but instead
went straight to his local girlfriend's house and moved in to stay. Craig had
completely turned his back on his family, his church, his mission agency,
his parents back home, his history, all except his job. It was devastating
news for all, to say the least.

It is, however, not a new story. Regrettably, it is a rather typical story
of those making the journey from rural to urban and losing all they got. It
is also the story of Lot, Abraham's nephew. Initially, Lot wanted to move
in the direction of Zoar because he "saw that the Jordan Valley was well
watered everywhere like the garden of the Lord" (Genesis 13:10). But Lot
ended up settling "among the cities of the valley and moved his tent as
far as Sodom" (v. 12). This did not bode well, as "the men of Sodom were
wicked, great sinners against the Lord" (v. 13). In contrast, Abraham built
an altar to the Lord (v. 18).

Twice Abraham intervenes on behalf of his nephew, getting him and
his family out of trouble. First, Lot got caught up in a regional tribal
feud and his family ended up being taken captive by Sodom's enemies.
Abraham gathered over 300 of his own trained men and rescued Lot's
family, the people, and the plunder, and returned them all to their cities.

The second time, a more infamous story, the Lord and two angels
appear to Abraham, warning him of the looming destruction of Sodom
and Gomorrah. Abraham negotiates with the Lord for the rescue of Lot
and his family, which the angels carry out, but not without losses. Lot's
future sons-in-law wouldn't hear any of it and refused to leave the city.
Lot's wife also felt the pull of the city and didn't make it far outside the
gate before turning around and turning into a pillar of salt. At the end

of Lot's story, only his two daughters survive, who then got their father drunk in order to have intercourse with him and produce children.

There is nothing about Lot's story that is redeemable, except to say, "Do not follow their example!" Yet, many families make the same mistake, lured by the apparent prosperity and freedom of the city. All good intentions come to naught and instead the family is swallowed up by the surrounding evil and inner lust. Lot had become one of the city leaders, sitting at the gate (the seat of government then), but he had no influence. Sadly, I have seen Christian and missionary families come to my city with all their good intentions, hoping to be of influence, but losing it all as a result of sin. Therefore, I say, "Once the city influences you more than you influence the city, get out right away!"

Not coincidentally, sandwiched between these two stories of Lot's disaster and Sodom's demise is an alternative story of a prototype city and an archetype king. It is just a glimpse and it is easy to miss. If it hadn't been for the author of Hebrews, who had caught a mysterious phrase in the Psalms, perhaps none would have ever caught the significance. It is the story of Melchizedek, the king of Salem. Next to nothing is known about this mystery man, but the little that is known is summarized as follows:

> *This Melchizedek was king of Salem and priest of God Most High. He met Abraham returning from the defeat of the kings and blessed him, and Abraham gave him a tenth of everything. First, the name Melchizedek means "king of righteousness"; then also, "king of Salem" means "king of peace." Without father or mother, without genealogy, without beginning of days or end of life, resembling the Son of God, he remains a priest forever. Just think how great he was: Even the patriarch Abraham gave him a tenth of the plunder!* (Hebrews 7:1-4)

Hebrews' author connects the dots between Melchizedek and Jesus based on Psalm 110:4, "The Lord has sworn and will not change his mind: 'You are a priest forever after the order of Melchizedek.'" Salem's king was a prefiguration of the Prince of Peace. The "king of righteousness," which is the meaning of the Hebrew *melchi-zedek*, foreshadowed Christ, the

Righteous King. Salem, the name of the city over which Melchizedek was king, is from the Hebrew word *shalom*, most often translated as "peace." The principle is this: When righteousness reigns over the city, the city is at peace. In the absence of righteousness (crime, injustice, sin, war), so peace will be absent from the city. Thus, a city aiming to be at peace and for peace must first tackle the problem of unrighteousness. It is only when Jesus Christ, the Prince of Peace and Righteous King, reigns over a city, that the city will be able to experience perfect shalom peace.

Shalom is both simple and complex to define. Shalom is a holistic peace, wholeness in the true sense of the word, something that the English *peace* falls short of. Therefore, shalom has been translated with a variety of words. For example, in Jeremiah 29:7 it is translated as "peace and prosperity" (NIV, NLT), "welfare" (ESV, NLT), "well-being" (MSG), and traditionally "peace" (KJV).

In *Walking with the Poor: Principles and Practices of Transformational Development,* Bryant Myers defines shalom as essentially relational, standing for peace in relation to "God, others, self and nature."[58] Shalom "means just relationships (living justly and experiencing justice), harmonious relationships and enjoyable relationships."[59] Shalom is the full and abundant life Jesus referred to in John 10:10.[60] The diagram in Figure 10 reflects this kind of relational and abundant shalom life.

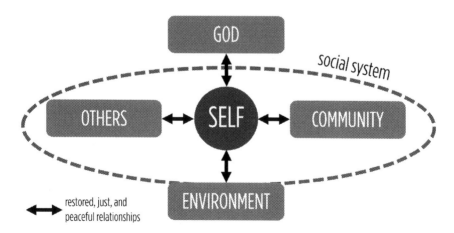

Figure 10. Transformed Relationships[61]

Human flourishing is a more recent term used to communicate the meaning of shalom across religious boundaries.[62] In *Urban Shalom and the Cities We Need,* Andre Van Eymeren introduces the concept of shalom as human flourishing. Van Eymeren states that shalom is "the well-being of the individual in the context of their community," which "encompasses everything necessary for healthful living" and should be seen as "completeness, wholeness or wellbeing in the present."[63]

In stark contrast with Lot and Sodom, Melchizedek and Salem introduce the first biblical perspective of God's vision for the city: The City of Shalom. This theme is carried forward into the next book of the Bible, in the Exodus story, and plays itself out in subsequent books in the form of David's city, Jerusalem. But the City of God finds its origins in an unlikely place: a refugee camp in the Sinai desert.

Done constructing cities for Egypt's Pharaoh, the Israelites narrowly escaped the king's clutches by God's mighty hand. An estimated two million people crossed the bottom of the Red Sea into the Sinai desert where they encamped in tents. In comparison, the recent Rohingya refugee crisis resulted in a camp of one million people inside Bangladesh, dubbed "the largest refugee camp in the world."[64] Bidi Bidi, one of the world's largest refugee camps, is being turned into a city of one-million people.[65] Israel's camp, sectioned by the 12 tribes of Jacob, the refugee settlement would qualify to be called a "mobile city."

It is at the center of the Exodus camp that we find the origins of Jerusalem, the City of God. At the heart of this mobile city is the Tabernacle structure, furnishings, and system, the place where humanity finds shalom with God. Out of that relationship, all other relationships (with self, others, community, environment) are restored and transformed. As noted earlier, we can draw a direct line from the garden to the Tabernacle to the New Jerusalem.

Yet, it will take another ten generations, over 400 years, until David's city is eventually established, and the Tabernacle is centered at the heart of the city God had chosen to put His name (1 Kings 11:36). Eventually it is Solomon who constructs Israel's temple, where God's presence and glory would have dwelled indefinitely were it not for the downfall of Israel's rulers, priests, and people.

No doubt Jerusalem was to be the model city, the heart of the nation, and the center of peace for the world. The name literally means, "the foundation of shalom," and is traditionally thought to have been the city of Salem over which Melchizedek was king. However, the books of the Kings, the Chronicles, and the prophets all attest to the waywardness of Israel's royalty, priesthood and citizens alike.

Again, the *awr* goes miserably awry! They worshiped idols, sacrificed their children in fire, shed innocent blood, oppressed the marginalized, increased the wealth of the rich, dishonored the boundaries of the clans, discontinued the Sabbath Year and the Year of Jubilee (if ever they had been celebrated), thereby refusing to return property to rightful owners and restore freedom to bondservants. With hindsight, Ezekiel prophesied, "Now this was the sin of your sister Sodom: She and her daughters were arrogant, overfed and unconcerned; they did not help the poor and needy." Jerusalem had done even worse and failed miserably to be the foundation of shalom.

The prophets started to predict the coming Messiah-king in the line of David who would restore all things. At the same time, the prophets also painted a picture of God's vision for the city, the heavenly model, the New Jerusalem. Zechariah proclaims:

> *This is what the Lord Almighty says: "Once again men and women of ripe old age will sit in the streets of Jerusalem, each of them with cane in hand because of their age. The city streets will be filled with boys and girls playing there." This is what the Lord Almighty says: "It may seem marvelous to the remnant of this people at that time, but will it seem marvelous to me?" declares the Lord Almighty.* (Zechariah 8:4-6)

Indeed, I marvel at this vision! God's city of shalom has space for children to safely play on the streets and for elderly to enjoy watching them. In my city, there is a dire lack of public and green space (only one square meter per person).[66] It would seem marvelous to me, and to all the Hanoians I share this verse with, if God's vision for the city would become a reality in Hanoi. Just thinking about all that would have to change in culture and infrastructure to make this a reality is mind blowing. If God indeed cares so much about public space for children and elderly, for safety and joy, shouldn't we Christians need to do something about it? This passage gives support for churches to build public playgrounds as their contribution towards a city of peace.

Through the prophet Isaiah, God further describes His vision for the peaceable city. In chapter 65:17-25 God presents several key components of what the New Jerusalem would include, which Ray Bakke highlights in his book *A Theology as Big as the City*.[67]

- ❑ Public celebrations and happiness (v. 17-25)
- ❑ Public health for children and aged (v. 20)
- ❑ Housing for all (v. 21)
- ❑ Food for all (v. 22)
- ❑ Family support systems (v. 23)
- ❑ Absence of violence (v. 25)

Jeremiah, "the weeping prophet," lived through the downfall of Jerusalem, its destruction, the ethnic cleansing at the hands of the Babylonians, and even the brutal murders which took place in the city among those left behind. No wonder the deep grief and loud cry composed in Lamentation's poetry—a cry later reverberated by Jesus as He laments over the city once more in foreknowledge of its final destruction. If only we too could express such deep lament over the crime and corruption in our cities.

Still, not all was lost. God would give the remnant in exile a second chance, but first they were to refocus and put into practice that which they had failed to do in the first place: to build, to settle, to plant, to multiply, to "seek the shalom of the city to which I [God] have carried you into exile and to pray to the Lord for it, because as it experiences shalom, you too will have shalom" (Jeremiah 29:7, paraphrase mine). Can you hear the echoes of the Creation Mandate? Do you see the pattern of Israel's previous life in Egypt? Can you catch the calling of the church in the First Century Roman Empire and the 21st Century globalized world?

It is hard for us to imagine how unfathomable this command must have seemed to the exiled remnant, though if you would tell Jerusalem's orthodox Jews today to seek the shalom of Bagdad, they probably would give you the same look Jeremiah might have received. It is this passage that sets us up for our posture as Christians in the city, but that is for the next chapter to uncover. For now, it is during the post-exilic period that a vision of the kingdom of God takes shape, which eventually takes form in the coming of Christ, and finally becomes reality at Christ's return.

A Theology of the Kingdom

When the kingdom of Israel was lost, the kingdom of God was found. Young Daniel was one of "the best of the best," taken from Jerusalem during the first siege, to be trained in Babylon's court for service to King Nebuchadnezzar. He remained there until the return of the Jewish exiles 70 years later. After one year into his new job, which was most challenging to the say the least, the king had a frightening dream no one could interpret except Daniel. The dream of a statue made of four kinds of materials, to finally be crushed by a mountain rock, pointed to four empires yet to come only to be overtaken by the kingdom of God. The rock in the dream that "became a huge mountain and filled the whole earth," referred to God's kingdom which "will itself endure forever" (Daniel 2:35,44). Nebuchadnezzar responded in awe and promoted Daniel to governor of Babylon province.

Fifty years into his exile, Daniel also had a dream. As the Jewish political advisor to the king of Babylon, Daniel experienced ups and downs in his career. Nebuchadnezzar had been unpredictable, to say the least. Now his successor, Belshazzar, proved to be even more vile and vain. It was soon after this change in government that Daniel had a troubling dream of four beasts. The dream concluded with a vision of the Ancient of Days seated upon a throne on judgment day and of "one like a son of man" receiving "authority, glory and sovereign power," being worshiped by "all nations and peoples of every language," whose dominion would be everlasting and whose kingdom would never be destroyed (7:14).

Daniel's interpretation of the king's dream, together with the interpretation given to Daniel for his dream, have proven to be very insightful. With hindsight, scholars today recognize the four major empires preceding the coming of Christ, namely Babylonia, Med-Persia, Greece, and Rome. How destructive, oppressive, and terrifying these empires would turn out to be, one after the other would fall until God's kingdom would finally crush them all to dust and spread throughout the world. God had said that He "blows on [the rulers of this world] and they wither, and a whirlwind sweeps them away like chaff" (Isaiah 40:24). A humbling experience for rulers like Nebuchadnezzar, yet a reassuring word for Daniel and the people of God.

The "son of man" in Daniel's dream would rule and reign this kingdom for eternity, being worshiped by people of all nations, tribes and languages. As Isaiah had prophesied, "Of the greatness of his government and [shalom] there will be no end. He will reign on David's throne and over his kingdom, establishing and upholding it with justice and righteousness from that time on and forever" (Isaiah 9:7).

It is on this note that Jesus starts His ministry, announcing the arrival of the "son of man" and His kingdom. It is also what got Him killed. Matthew kicks off Jesus' ministry with Him preaching, "Repent, for the kingdom of heaven has come near" (Matthew 4:17). At the end, Jesus is charged with blasphemy as He declares to the Sanhedrin, "From now on you will see the Son of Man sitting at the right hand of the Mighty One and coming on the clouds of heaven" (Matthew 26:64). When Pontius Pilate asks Jesus, "Are you the king of the Jews?" Jesus answers affirmative, "You have said so" (Matthew 27:11).

Jesus' claim to the kingdom and the kingship are the bookends of the gospel. He did not preach a gospel of spiritual salvation for the soul to spend eternity in an ethereal heaven. Jesus came "proclaiming the good news of the kingdom, and healing every disease and sickness among the people" (Matthew 4:23). Both the spiritual and physical reality of God's kingdom had arrived in Jesus—heaven had come to earth. As in Daniel's vision and Isaiah's prophecies, the extent and expanse of this kingdom would know no bounds.

Early on in Jesus' ministry, Luke records Jesus preaching in His home synagogue in Nazareth. Reading from Isaiah 61:1-2, Jesus stated:

"The Spirit of the Lord is on me,
because he has anointed me
to proclaim good news to the poor.
He has sent me to proclaim freedom for the prisoners
and recovery of sight for the blind,
to set the oppressed free,
to proclaim the year of the Lord's favor." (Luke 4:18-19)

Clearly, the gospel of the kingdom is not just one of salvation, but also of salvaging. It is the good news of the restoration of all things gone awry, of the recovery of the rights and freedom of society's marginalized, of the reinstatement of the year of Jubilee to bring equity for all. Wherever Jesus went was the kingdom's extent. It is this kingdom authority, which had been given to Him, that He passed on to His followers. First to the 12, then to the 72, and finally to all present at His ascension.

"All authority in heaven and on earth has been given to me. Therefore go and make disciples of all nations, baptizing them in the name of the Father and of the Son and of the Holy Spirit, and teaching them to obey everything I have commanded you. And surely I am with you always, to the very end of the age." (Matthew 28:18-20)

Surprising to us, the disciples knew nothing about church, church planting, church management, church denominations, or church multiplication. The English word *church* come from the German word *kirche*, which refers to a church building. The Greek word *ecclesia*, which has been translated to church, has nothing to do with a building, but everything with the gathering, assembly, or meeting of God's people. The word *ecclesia* was used for a townhall meeting in which the community would decide over the management of the town and stewardship over the environment.

Johannes Reimer points out that God's purpose for the *ecclesia* is to reinstate the authority of God's people over all creation and every nation.

"Ecclesia in the view of Jesus is a community of people *called out of the world to accept responsibility for the world.*"[68] Sadly, over the centuries, the *ecclesia* became more about church buildings, church structures, church denominations, and church dogma. E. Stanley Jones argues that this is why communism took a hold in Christian Orthodox Russia, because the church leaders were too busy arguing about the colors of their robes while the poor were out of work and out of food. Communism at least provided answers to the problem of the oppression of the poor by the rich and promised an alternative idealism to the hierarchical orthodoxy of the state sanctioned church.[69]

It is a good thing that the disciples didn't know anything about church or about the troubles church leaders would create in the next two millennia. After Jesus' resurrection, He kept teaching them about the kingdom of God and the power of the Holy Spirit which would enable them to be witnesses to the ends of the world. So on they went "proclaim[ing] the kingdom of God and [teaching] about the Lord Jesus Christ" (Acts 28:31, see also 8:12, 19:8, 20:25, 28:23). It has always been about the King and His kingdom.

Remarkably, though it should not surprise us, the city has a primary role in this kingdom expansion program. The 120 or so believers who had gathered on the day of Pentecost, waiting for the outpouring of the Spirit as Jesus had instructed them, were in the upper room when wind and fire came upon them. Speaking in the languages of all the nations, the curse of Babel reversed in Jerusalem. By the end of the day, 3,000 Jewish believers from across the empire were added to their number. Revival had broken out in the city, the curse of Babel had been canceled, and the seeds of the kingdom had been sown into the Jewish diaspora across the world. Only in global urban centers can such impact take place!

Maybe it was because the management of an instant megachurch kept the disciples busy, but it took persecution to move Philip and Peter to extend the kingdom to the cities of Judea and Samaria. Still, their Jewishness kept them from crossing cultural boundaries, even after Cornelius' conversion. It wasn't until some expatriate believers started talking to Greeks in Rome's western capital city that the nations caught on fire. It was the international church in Antioch, not the national church in Jerusalem, that became the springboard for reaching the ends of the earth.

Within a time span of 25 years, Paul and his team had "proclaimed of the kingdom of God and taught about the Lord Jesus Christ" in most prominent cities across the empire. The new believers formed simple *ecclesia* gatherings, appointing elders to provide oversight, and were networked with one another through an exchange of circular letters and interchange of expatriate workers and traveling missionaries. It was the global diaspora, common language, transportation infrastructure, and urban centers that provided the means for the Holy Spirit to make this rapid expansion possible. This is still true today.

At the end of the biblical narrative, in the final two chapters of Revelation, the four strands of city, place, shalom, and kingdom come together and unite. What began in a garden, the first Holy of Holies, ends in the city, the final Holy of Holies. The nations march into the cities and bring with them all that is good from their cultures as gifts for the King. God finally dwells with all His people from every nation, tribe and tongue. Heaven has come to earth, the Groom has come to the Bride, and all are joined as one. The City of Peace as designed by the Great Architect makes a place on earth for shalom to prevail and the King of kings to reign.

This is how I see these biblical principles intertwine throughout Scripture and find their final integration in the new creation (see Figure 11). It not only informs us how we think about our cities and our mission, but also about how we posture ourselves to those around, below, and above us.

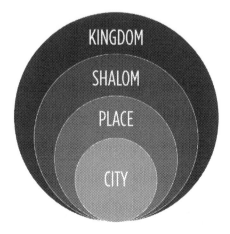

Figure 11: The four theologies in relation to each other

CHAPTER 5

POSTURE

"By this everyone will know that you are my disciples,
if you love one another."

John 13:35

I was really, really nervous. The international reception hall seemed filled with police uniforms. It was the first time I visited Hanoi's Chief of Police, Major General Nguyen Duc Chung. With me were Pastor Nelson Annan (Canadian), Pastor Jinggoy Caballero (Filipino), and Pastor Paul Bui (Vietnamese, who acted as my translator). With the chief were the head of Hanoi security police (like the FBI), officers of the religious department of the city police, and a handful of other policemen and -women.

It was not the first time I had found myself meeting with uniformed police. In 2012, I had met with the General overseeing the Protestant office of the religious department of Hanoi police. Entering the Police Headquarters and being guided to a small office with uniformed officers, I was quite nervous then too! Gratefully, I had remembered what I had learned from the Love Boulder story, when the pastors had asked Boulder's mayor how they could love their city.[70] Thus, after introductions and a short speech by the General on the freedom of religion in Vietnam, it was my turn to speak. This is what I said,

> Many foreigners come to Hanoi for their own career or for their company's profit, but we tell our church members to love Hanoi and to contribute to society while they are here. How can we as Christian foreigners love Hanoi better?

The General was puzzled by my question and was quiet for a while. His response was that we would be welcome to contribute to society and could work with the relevant government offices. Only afterwards did I learn that when the General had given me the opportunity to speak, the expectation was that I would have made a formal request for his favor, as a beneficiary would ask from a benefactor. I could have asked for permission or rights or privileges, but instead I had asked how we foreigners could love his city better. Two years later, I asked the Chief of Police the same question: "How can we love Hanoi?" Again, I did not ask for permits, rights, or favors.

Since we launched the Love Hanoi campaign, whenever I would meet with government officials, I would always ask the same question, "How can we love Hanoi?" We would give the officials Love Hanoi promotional products (mugs, pens, notebooks, bags, etc.) and slowly but surely HIF became known for loving Hanoi. It is a good reputation to have, since Jesus had said, "By this everyone will know that you are my disciples, if you love one another" (John 13:35).

It is this posture of unconditional love towards the city and civil government that has helped me overcome my own fears and prejudices. Our shared goal of loving Hanoi has made it possible for us to build mutual trust and understanding. It has helped our church not to appear as if we have a covert secret agenda, but to have one agenda: to love God, people, and the city! It has helped our church members to actively seek the shalom of the city and to pray for its transformation. Along the way, the government invited HIF to register our church and our worship facility, and even provided us with missionary visas for our staff! "Give, and you will receive," Jesus had said (Luke 6:38, NLT). Praise be to God!

For this paradigm shift to take place, I first had to personally be transformed in my beliefs about my role and the role of the church in the city. This then led to a posture of being a blessing to the city, wanting to contribute to society, and focusing on building community. My posture had to shift from being an expatriate expert to becoming a local learner, from being church-centric to becoming kingdom-oriented, from being a consumer of the city to becoming a contributor to society, from viewing mission through a dichotomous lens to using a lens of shalom-peace, from *doing for* the city to *working with* the city and its government.

That is quite a list of shifts, and I could probably name a few more, but I will focus on four topics in this chapter. First, I will discuss two typical postures we may find churches to have towards the city, namely the church-centric posture and the church-escape posture. I will then expound on the posture of the church as part of the city. Second, I will unpack the posture of the church towards the city, exploring the model of Christ-Centered Civic Renewal and its five elements. Third, I will delve into the posture of the church towards their local community, drawing from ancient and modern concepts of the local parish. Finally, I will dig deeper into the posture towards the poor and what it means to serve with a posture of being "poor in spirit."

POSTURES OF THE CHURCH

As a pastor, it is very hard not to be church-centric in my thinking, planning, and ministry. Sunday is always coming, congregational needs are ever present, volunteer roles continually have to be filled, finances are often short, vision consistently is leaking, systems and processes keep on breaking down, and programs constantly dwindle. I often feel like the little Dutch boy who put his finger in the dike to keep Haarlem from flooding.[71] Since a boy's little finger won't stop a dike from bursting, it often feels pointless, because a leak will spring up somewhere else. Have you ever felt this way?

As we have discovered in the previous chapter, the theological principles of the church contributing to the city are sound. But to ask pastors to turn their attention outwards, and to also be attentive to the myriad of needs in their community and city, is asking for quite a lot! Yet, we must. If our churches are ever to be missionally engaged in our given context, pastors must lead the way. However, this is not a typical posture of pastors and churches towards their city. Most likely they have not been taught such theology and skills in seminary.

Historically, evangelicals have separated themselves from society in the past century. In a counter reaction to the liberal and socially oriented

movements in mainline Protestant churches, evangelical churches resorted
to fundamentalism and separatism. After World War II, evangelical
spirituality became more internally focused with a future orientation
towards the kingdom of God. Salvation was for the individual soul
to eventually go to heaven after death. Between salvation and death,
worshipful experiences became the focus (and the reason for hopping
from one church to another to find a better experience). Outreach was
oriented around evangelistic activities that led to the salvation of other
souls and the growth of the church. Church growth, therefore, became
the metric for success. It was completely possible (and sadly acceptable)
that cities in the Global North as well as in the South could be populated
with a Christian majority and countless churches, but still be worse off in
crime, pollution, and unemployment.[72]

I am intentionally overstating reality, as many evangelicals have also
been engaged in society, social work, and governance. However, typically
the view of church's posture towards society have fallen into two categories:
The church ruling the city (see Figure 12), and the church escaping the
city (see Figure 13).[1]

Figure 12: The church-centric posture[73]

---

[1]   H. Spees, cofounder of the Leadership Foundation, developed these two models in
his dissertation, *Christ Centered Civic Renewal* (2012).

THE CHURCH-CENTRIC POSTURE is that of the church ruling the city. The church wants to play a controlling role within the city and society, or else it will not participate. It is easy to detect such attitudes when speaking with pastors. If the church (and their church specifically) cannot be at the center of things, control the program, or benefit from the resources expensed, interest is quickly lost. In the conversation, the topic will always circle around their church. Why should their church spend money to help the poor if they cannot evangelize them and give an altar call? Why should their church partner with other churches if the risk is that the other church will receive more converts? If their church cannot grow as a result of the proposed project, why participate? It is a church-centric posture, which can be perceived as being condemning and judgmental by society and even by other churches and pastors.

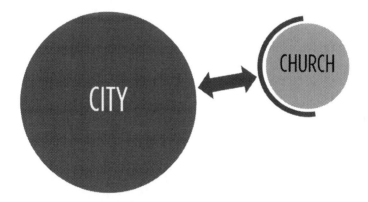

Figure 13: The church-escape posture[74]

THE CHURCH-ESCAPE POSTURE is that of the church escaping the city. It is a separatist approach where the church is holy and sacred, and the city is sinful and secular. The church feels that it is their responsibility to attack society and government, putting themselves in a position of defending their rights, beliefs, and freedoms. Getting involved in society would risk getting stained with the sin of the city (or getting the carpet stained). Christians should not get involved in politics because it implies compromising their faith. Outreach would be done *to* the city and *for* the lost. "Taking our cities for Christ" or other militaristic lingo is utilized by churches outside the city. The impression other churches and society have of churches with this separatist posture is that they are compassionless and arrogant. Neither the church-escape posture nor the church-centric glorify Christ in the city. The church needs to see itself integrated as part of the city (see Figure 14).

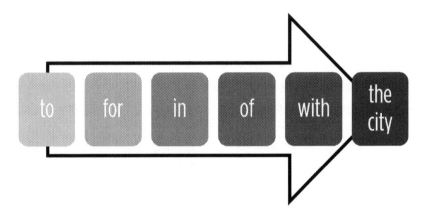

Figure 14: The church-integral posture

THE CHURCH-INTEGRAL POSTURE is that of the church seeing itself as an essential and indispensable part of the city. The escapist church sees itself going *to* the city doing things *for* the city to conquer the city (or at least to save some people from the city). The centric church sees itself being *in* the city doing things *for* the city to control the city. What should happen instead is that the church needs to shift from going *to* the city, doing things *for* the city, or just being *in* the city, to becoming the church as a part *of* the city and working together *with* the city.

I can relate to this shift in posture from my own personal experience. For the first decade of Hanoi International Fellowship, the church was made up of only expatriates who had come *to* the city. In those days, Hanoi was considered a "hardship posting" for diplomats, but we all felt it, whether or not we got a hardship bonus! As a church, we had no relationship with city government, but we would sponsor small projects our members were doing *for* the city. When I started as the pastor of HIF in 2005, we had come to realize that we are a church *in* the city. We needed to repent from our escapist posture and become outwardly oriented. It was not until we launched the Love Hanoi campaign that we started to see ourselves as an integral part *of* the city, a church working *with* the city. With a growing theology of the city, placemaking, shalom, and kingdom, we came to realize that we can work together across society's sectors through our common values.

Posture Towards the City

Seeing the church as an integral part of the city and a contributor towards the shalom-peace of society opens all kinds of opportunities to serve Christ and demonstrate His love across organizational, denominational, institutional, and sectoral boundaries. It is a humbling realization that the church as an institution (i.e. the Church citywide) is only one part of the non-profit sector, along with other religious and charitable groups. Furthermore, it will require collaboration with these groups and other institutions across the public and private sectors to truly "seek the peace and prosperity of the city" (see Figure 15).

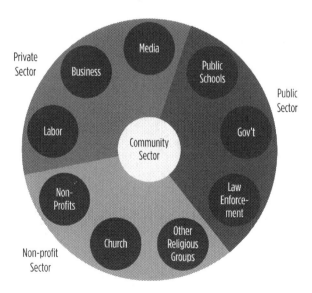

Figure 15: The church as part of the city[75]

One pastor who models how Christians can work together with other faith groups is Bob Roberts. Senior Pastor of Northwood Church, Roberts proudly refers to his partnership with a Jewish rabbi and a Muslim diplomat as "the three amigos." Founder of the Global Faith Forum,[m] Bob has created an open platform for leaders of different faiths to share thoughts, ideas, and experiences for the benefit of society. When I attended the first GFF conference at Northwood Church, I was deeply impressed by Bob's posture toward other faith leaders. He would be up front and say that because he loves his friends so much and wants to spend eternity with them, he would like to baptize them if he could! At the same time, Bob would respect and honor his fellow religious leaders on the shared platform, even though it was his church. They shared stories of how they collaborated in their respective cities and countries for the betterment of society. It is exactly in these open relationships, in this kind of collaboration for the benefit of the city, that we find the greatest opportunities to be salt and light for the Father's glory. If the church remains controlling or defensive, those opportunities would be lost, and the Father's name would likely be tainted.

In many instances, especially in pre- and post-Christian nations, the church is only a small minority. In Hanoi, Protestant Evangelical Christians make up only 0.1% of the population. Yet, Jesus told us that we *"are* the salt of society" and that we *"are* the light of the world." Spreading the salt and shining the light through our "good deeds" *will* "glorify [our] Father in heaven" (see Matthew 5:13-16, emphasis mine). Therefore, let's get the salt out of the saltshaker and the light from underneath the shades and give God glory through works that are good, right, beautiful, and excellent!

The beauty is that, no matter the percentage, the church is *already* present in the city through five different venues:

1. **CONGREGATIONS:** The church is present through local congregations in their communities, through formal church buildings or non-traditional gathering places in schools, homes, and other rented facilities.

2. **INSTITUTIONS:** The church is present as a citywide institution. The more the church unites for the benefit of the city, the greater its visible and felt presence.

---

[m] Check out www.globalfaithforum.com/bob-roberts-jr

3. **DOMAINS:** The church is present in each of the institutions across the sectors because of the jobs Christians hold in their domains. They are teachers, government employees, and policemen and -women; they are working in media, businesses, and manufacturing; they already serve communities through their non-profit initiatives.

4. **CONNECTORS:** The church is actively working for the city's benefit through connectors, Christians who are gifted and called to build bridges between the institutions for the benefit of their communities and the city (see Figure 16).

5. **INTERCESSORS:** The church is present through prayer. Christians can spiritually intercede for segments and sections of the city without being physically present, whether at home or during their church service or in prayer gatherings. At the same time, praying while being physically present through prayer walking is a powerful strategy to observe the kingdom of light and the kingdom of darkness at work at the street level while praying for the heaven's kingdom to prevail.[76]

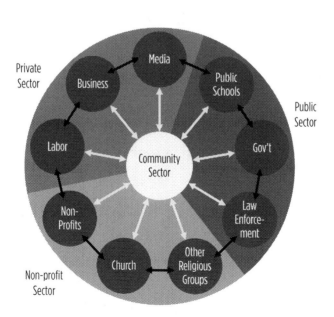

Figure 16: Cross sector collaboration for the benefit of the city[77]

This model of the church as part of the city was developed by H. Spees and is called *Christ-Centered Civic Renewal* (CCCR). A second model developed by Spees is the Five Elements of CCCR, which are: Church Unity, Leadership Humility, Civil Society, Embracing Spirituality, and Community Development.[78] As shown in Figure 17, this model can be viewed from both the horizontal relationship between church and city (the Public/ Institutional Dimension), and the vertical relationship between leadership and spirituality (the Personal/Individual Dimension).

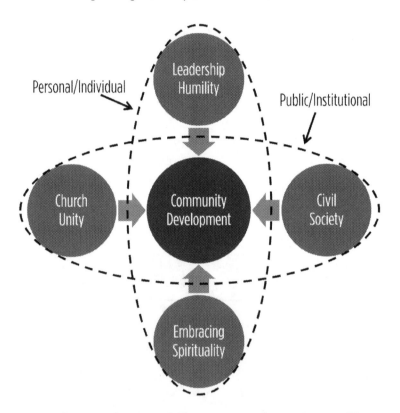

Figure 17: The Five Elements of Christ-Centered Civic Renewal[79]

Taking the horizontal dimension into consideration, Spees makes the following observation, which I copy here in its entirety because of its importance:

In a sense, the relationship between the City and the Church is what sets the playing field for CCCR. Both City and Church are "quantitative factors" in that they bring physical, measurable personnel, financial, facilities, and other resources to the table ... The tension is between two powers: on one hand, the power of a system that seeks to derive its purpose, mission, and authority from God (Church) versus, on the other hand, the power of a system that seeks to derive its purpose, mission, and authority from people (City). The common purpose is the common good, especially when considered at the margins, among the most vulnerable. Because, in truth, the Church is a subset of the City, CCCR practitioners who accept this reality understand that *the responsibility is on the Church to first establish within itself the type of relationships that lead to unity of purpose and then to serve the City. When the Church brings its resources to the table of service for the common good, especially with and among the poor and vulnerable, the tension is reduced.* When the Church sets itself above or in place of the City, the tension is increased and the hope for human development is diminished. The City, like the Church, is at its best when it pursues a common vision among its various institutions among which is the Church. Building a culture of community around the pursuit of the common good is basic to all democratic principles.[80]

Note the two italicized sentences. First, it is vital for the Church to unite around the common purpose of seeking the shalom of the city. If the Church wants to be taken seriously by city government, we first must unite and form an institutional unit, even if only as an informal and relational network. Second, with an attitude to work together for the common good of the city, it reduces the tension between City and Church. These tensions of mistrust and misunderstanding between Church and City is present in most cities around the world, not just in Hanoi or in your city. This tension is also two-way, where the Church mistrusts city government and vice versa. More likely than not, this is with good reason, and efforts of reconciliation must take place to (re)build trust and understanding. To reduce such tensions and improve relationships with the City, the Church must adopt a posture of seeking the common good, i.e. to seek the shalom of the city through action and prayer (Jeremiah 29:7).

When I read Spees' dissertation in 2013, I realized how much the horizontal relationship between Church and City was needed in Hanoi. God had already been working to increase fellowship and collaboration among the church leaders to bring citywide church unity. For me, Spees' model was prophetic insight and foresight to see the critical nature of this horizontal relationship. It urged me to invest time and energy in building unity among church leaders and fostering mutual understanding with city government. The CCCR model inspired me to choose the phrase, "Joining Hands for the Benefit of the Community," as the initial slogan for the Love Hanoi campaign. In Vietnamese the phrase is culturally meaningful, "Chung tay vì Lợi ích Cộng đồng." (Later the slogan was updated to a shorter phrase, "Building Community Together.")

Looking at the vertical dimension of the Five Elements of CCCR, Spees highlights the following:

> The relationship between Leadership and Spirituality is what endows CCCR with its unique power and vision. Both Leadership and Spirituality are "qualitative factors" in that they bring internal resources such as values, vision, and character to the process of CCCR. ... There is a vital relationship between the Church/City Horizontal Axis to the Leadership/Spirituality Vertical Axis. As was mentioned earlier, the horizontal axis represents a more quantitative aspect of CCCR, while the vertical represents a more qualitative aspect. Perhaps more significantly, the sheer institutional complexity and diversity and sometimes fragmentation within both the Church and the City can tend towards disintegration and a centrifugal pulling apart, while the coalescing powers of both leadership and spirituality tend toward integration and a centripetal pulling together.[81]

The citywide church is beautiful in its diversity of history and expression. Although often fragmented, it is humility in leadership that can pull the churches together as a citywide institution. At the same time, civic leaders need to take on a posture of humility as well to cross the boundaries between institutions for the benefit of the city's communities. Coupled with a spirituality that is embracing of others, this type of collaborative effort becomes unstoppable.

Embracing others does not mean agreeing with everything the other person stands for but accepting them as they are. Jesus was a star at this, having meals with tax collectors and with religious leaders alike, answering prayers of both the Roman Centurion and the repentant sinner, forgiving both the Samaritan woman who had divorced five times and the adulterous woman who had been condemned to death. To be honest, Jesus embraced people I would be very uncomfortable with!

Spees separates personal spirituality from the institutional Church for a purpose. Drawing from N.T. Wright, Miroslav Volf, and Catholic Social Teaching, Spees extrapolates what he calls "The Downward Call." Philippians 2:1-11 describes how followers of Christ should adopt the attitude of Christ and lay down their lives for others. This downward movement of Christ, which is echoed in numerous other passages, eventually led to His resurrection and exaltation. "The downward call leads to renewal," says Spees, which is reflected in each of the five CCCR elements: humility, common good, embracing, faith, and unity all lead to community development.

Spees pulls the five elements together in a brief but poignant statement:

> CCCR invites people to listen and respond to the downward call leading to renewal, and in following that call finds strong biblical and theological foundation. CCCR finds people whose leadership humility, commitment to the common good, spirituality that embraces the other, and faith, placing unity ahead of agenda, positions them to focus on community development. The process results in engaging everyone in on-the-ground efforts that renew the city.[82]

This is where the rubber meets the road, so to speak. At the crux of urban community development is the call to lay down one's self and respond to the challenge with personal sacrifice. This personal commitment is what drives people, churches, and institutions to seek the peace of the community and the city.

POSTURE TOWARDS THE COMMUNITY

One formidable example of a humble and embracing spiritual leader is Father Ben Beltran of the Smokey Mountain community in Manila, Philippines. When Father Beltran moved to what was the largest garbage slum in the city, he made the slum his parish and viewed every person as a member of that parish. He started his ministry by asking everyone he met, "Who do you think Jesus is?" Beltran believed that, "No one will follow you unless you spend time with them, it is about relationships."[83] So he spent time with the members of his parish and asked a simple question. Through this exercise he discovered that Jesus was already present in the community. This personal research project eventually became the thesis of Beltran's doctoral degree and was later published in his book, *The Christology of the Inarticulate: An Inquiry into the Filipino Understanding of Jesus the Christ.*[84]

As a result of Father Beltran's ministry, Smokey Mountain today is no longer a garbage dump. Through collaborative efforts, Beltran and partners were able to transform the city's garbage collection and processing systems, launching their own businesses and recycling programs. Today, Veritas Social Empowerment, Inc. runs an IT school and other educational programs, taking an entrepreneurial approach to working with the poor. The company's slogan clearly states Beltran's vision and intent, "Imagine. Innovate. Impact."[85]

The unity of the church, humility of its leaders, and spirituality of its members very much depends on the posture of the pastor. Lowell Bakke poses a critical question: "Is [the pastor] a pastor in a church which happens to be *in* a community, or which is *for* a community?"[86] The answer to this question unveils what pastors think about their role in the city. Raineer Chu, attorney with Mission Ministries Philippines (MMP), challenges pastors to consider the posture of the Catholic priest. "Learn to journey with the poor, all other things become secondary," stated Chu.[87]

In coming to a community, as Father Beltran did, the comparison between a Catholic priest and an evangelical pastor provides quite a contrast in posture. Chu further explains,

> When entering the slum, a priest has a very graphic image of Jesus [as a statue] whereas a pastor has the image of Jesus' presence [ethereal]. A priest has a theology of God's presence everywhere. A priest comes to the community to find God there whereas the pastor goes to bring God. The priest in his order goes to grow old there, die there, and be buried there. Francis Schaeffer, in his books, says evangelicals have already "found" Jesus, whereas the orthodox have a great sense of journey. Pastors divide between members and non-members; the priest is called to the parish.[88]

Based on Chu's observations, the following table lists the contrasting postures of priest and pastor (see Table 1). Obviously, this is exaggerated and stereotyping, but I felt confronted by the stark contrast when Chu shared this comparison with my class in Manila. Looking at the table, I can certainly identify more with the pastor's posture than with the priest. Bringing God to the city while focused on accomplishing a project, moving fast, preaching, and opening lines of communication—all these are valid descriptors of me. Now I have a dilemma: I want to see the city as my parish, but to do so I need to constantly fight against my default posture towards the city as a typical evangelical pastor.

Table 1: Contrasting the Catholic priest and the evangelical pastor's posture towards the community[89]

PRIEST:	PASTOR:
Finding God in the community	Bringing God to the community
Sense of journey	Accomplishing a project
Walking slowly	Traveling fast
The whole community is the parish	Divides church members and non-members
Focus on the sick, poor, and dying	Focus on Scripture and communication

The Parish Collective is reviving the concept of parish in a post-Christendom context.[n] In their book, *The New Parish,* founders Paul Sparks, Tim Soerens and Dwight J. Friesen define the word "parish" as *"all the relationships (including the land) where the local church lives out its faith together."* Parish, they state, "is a unique word that recalls a geography large enough to live life together (live, work, play, etc.) and small enough to be known as a character within it."[90]

The *Merriam-Webster* dictionary defines *parish* as "the ecclesiastical unit of area committed to one pastor." Originating from Greek, the word "parish" meant *near* (para-) *house* (oikos), or in other words, a neighborhood or vicinity. In the 13th century, the word *diocese* became synonymous to it, meaning *thorough* (dia-) *house* (oikos). Today, city churches tend to be less local and more affinity based due to preference of denomination, worship style, preaching style, available programs, friendships, etc. *The New Parish* authors argue that the urban church must be present, rooted, and linked in the neighborhood so that it can also lead fellow parishioners (neighbors) into the kingdom.

> Your parish is a relational microcosm that helps bring many cause-and-effect relationships back together again. Being in collaborative relationships in real life (where you live, work, and play) awakens you to the effects of your actions both on people and on the place itself. It creates a context where your church can see whether its faith is more than just talk. The local place becomes the testing ground, revealing whether you have learned to love each other and the larger community around you. In essence, the parish is a dare to your faith.[91]

How is *The New Parish* different from the "old" version? The authors highlight three keynote revisions:[92]

- The neighborhood—in all its diversity—has a voice that contributes to the form of the church. There is a growing sense that the Spirit works through the relationships of the neighborhood

---

[n]   For more information, visit www.parishcollective.org

to teach us what love and faithfulness look like in that particular context.

- The way diverse church expressions with different names and practices are learning to live out their faith together as the unified church in and among the neighborhood.
- They seek out partnerships with people from the other faith perspectives who have common hopes for the neighborhood.

The New Parish has an integrated focus on community, formation, and mission. Present, rooted, and linked, the church partners with those in the parish to seek the common good of the community. The purpose of the church is "living out God's dream and caring for the place we are called."[93] Mission is not just something "out there," but also local ventures "right here." The new parish becomes a community discerning the Holy Spirit's leading for their purpose, reinventing itself as the parish transforms, and loving those in special interest groups so "that all might flourish."[94] Pastor and church members alike are committed to lead by example.

I have had the pleasure of having had conversations with Dwight Friesen, co-author of *The New Parish* and professor at the Seattle Institute for Theology and Psychology. When I stated that I feel called to the city as my parish and that my church is a city-church, he responded that this was impossible. My point, however, is that international churches are generally made up of people from across the world living across the city. Expatriates are truly global nomads, roaming the world from one urban context to the next. Usually staying for only two to three years, not enough time to learn language and culture, expats usually clique together around school, church, ethnic, or social communities.

Although "global citizens" is an idealized concept, expats are citizens of none with few ties to their passport culture. Can the city be a parish for expatriates? I believe international churches like HIF can help bridge the gap so foreign Christians can have a missional experience while they are temporary residents of their host city. What needs to be kept in front and center is "The Downward Call," as Spees called it, where expatriates realize their common poverty and are mindful of those with less.

Posture Towards the Poor

"Why did Jesus come to earth?" "For what specific sin(s) was Old Testament Israel sent into captivity?" "What is the primary task of the church?" The way these questions are answered have a profound impact on our posture towards the poor, according to Steve Corbett and Brian Fikkert in their book *When Helping Hurts*.[95] The easy answers would be: "Jesus came to save people from sin and death, the Israelites worshipped idols instead of God, and the church is to preach the gospel and make disciples of all nations." Though these statements are true, they are incomplete.

Jesus said that He had come "to proclaim good news to the poor ... freedom for the prisoners and recovery of sight for the blind, to set the oppressed free" (Luke 4:18). The Israelites were judged in part due to the injustices done to the poor, which is apparent from the prophetic writings. For example, in Ezekiel God judges Jerusalem for being worse than the sister-city of Sodom, who had sinned because she had been "arrogant, overfed and unconcerned; they did not help the poor and needy" (Ezekiel 16:48-49). The apostle Paul wrote to the Colossians that "God was pleased to have all his fullness dwell in [Jesus], and through him to reconcile to himself all things, whether things on earth or things in heaven, by making peace through his blood, shed on the cross" (Colossians 1:19-20). Jesus came not just save our souls for heaven, but to restore the poor, the prisoners, the blind, and the oppressed—and with them *all things* unto the Father. The task of the church is to continue this mission of Christ in bringing restoration to all things until the day of His return.

Looking at poverty from this perspective gives us a more holistic framework from which to serve the poor. Rather than focusing on material poverty, all mankind is poor in various ways and degrees. As illustrated in the previous chapter (see Figure 10), we all experience a level of poverty in our relationship with God (poverty of spiritual intimacy), with self (poverty of being), with others (poverty of community), and with the rest of creation (poverty of stewardship).[96] "Poverty is the result of relationships that do not work, that are not just, that are not for life, that are not harmonious or enjoyable," the authors quote. "Poverty is the absence of shalom in all its meaning."[97] The overall goal for material poverty alleviation, then, "is working to reconcile the four foundational relationships so that people can fulfill their callings of glorifying God by working and supporting themselves and their families with the fruit of that work."[98]

When working with the materially poor, helping is far more likely to hurt if we do not "embrace our mutual brokenness" and shared poverty.[99] Sin has caused distortions in mankind's relationships with God, creation, community, others, and self. We need to realize that "in God's sight all human beings are poor."[100] This includes the so-called 'non-poor' who also suffer from a marred identity in relation to God's image. The Lausanne Movement describes "the poverty of the rich" well:

> Consider the wealth of the poor. Materially poor people around the world demonstrate vibrancy, human strength, perseverance, ingenuity and unprecedented faith and joy—their dire circumstances and "wealth" often correlated. Consider, also, the poverty of the rich. Notice their search for meaning, their pursuit of decadence, their apathy. We also know our "imageness," rich and poor alike, is marred by the Fall. No one escapes brokenness and the need for redemption. We all need to be put back together again. We're all wealthy; we're all poor.[101]

Corbett and Fikkert felt the necessity to repent of the so-called "health and wealth gospel," which "teaches that God rewards increasing levels of faith with greater amounts of wealth."[102] The prosperity gospel places the blame of poverty on the lack of faith of the poor, whereas in fact the poor more often have far greater faith than the wealthy as they are forced to believe for God's provisions in daily bread and miraculous healing. "Poverty of the non-poor is harder to change,"[103] thus it is better to pray, "Give me neither poverty nor riches, but give me only my daily bread" (Proverbs 30:8).

One excellent example of how helping without hurting works is the ministry of Aaron Smith in the Botocan squatter community.[104] Located in Quezon City, a middle-class suburb of Manila Metro, Botocan is over 30 years old and more developed than other slums. With electricity, water, and concrete buildings (which were constructed after a fire had destroyed most of the shacks), families are settled, and young people feel at home. When asked if they would rather move out of the neighborhood, the residents said they'd prefer to stay in Botocan and could not imagine living elsewhere. The Filipino collectivistic culture of family and community prioritizes relationships over material wealth. Though materially poor, the people have a wealth in relationships with family, with the community, and (for the Christians) with God. The small house church Aaron worked with was rich with joy, love, and faith.

In this chapter we have stepped from Principles to Posture. A biblical theology *of* and *for* the city transforms our posture towards the city, the community, and the poor. Evangelical churches have tended to be either church-centric or church-escapist in their posture towards the city. The church needs to shift its posture from going *to* and doing *for* the city, to being *in* and *of* the city while working *with* the city. Christ-Centered Civic Renewal and its five elements presents a working model for churches to be missionally engaged in their cities. As leaders of churches, pastors also need to experience this paradigm shift and start seeing their church's community as their parish. Lessons can be learned from the old parish model of Catholicism while adopting the mindset of *The New Parish* of the Parish Collective. This poses challenges in particular for international churches and expatriates. All can be mindful of the poor, however, if a posture of mutual poverty is adopted. "Blessed are the poor in spirit," Jesus said, "for they will inherit the kingdom of heaven." Indeed, the materially poor can be wealthier in joy, hope, love, and faith.

How then do churches and Christians go about missionally engaging their communities? That question takes us to the next step of citywide movements: Process.

CHAPTER 6

PROCESS

"In the same way, let your light shine before others, that they may see your good deeds and glorify your Father in heaven."

Matthew 5:16

In the early '70s, Naim Ateek had come to Saudi Arabia as a little boy. His parents were among the thousands of refugees who had fled the Lebanese civil war. Through contacts in Jordan, they ended up in Riyadh, Saudi's capital city.

Naim turned out to be a brilliant student and quickly made it to the top of the class. He was soon recruited by Saudi's largest oil company. Through hard work, diligence, and a succession of promotions, Naim ended up in one of the company's top positions. As the VP of Security and Finance, he had a very influential position, often working closely with the company's president. This had its benefits, although the president could be very temperamental and unpredictable. Naim had to constantly be on his guard when in the president's presence.

One night, while staying at the company's luxurious resort, Naim flipped on the news after a long and grueling day of meetings. The TV program suddenly caught his attention. The news reporter was covering a story of the current state of Lebanon, his country of birth. Naim couldn't remember the last time he had given a thought to his homeland.

Now, however, the images on the screen tugged at this heart. Children needed schools and medicine. Homes were still riddled with holes from the shooting and bombing years ago. Life in Beirut was dangerous; most people preferred to live in villages. In that moment, Naim saw his own life flash before him. He had come from rags to riches and now had everything he could ever want. Yet his own people were in dire need of even the most basic things. Suddenly he realized that he was in a position to make a difference.

With that overwhelming thought, Naim broke down and wept. He had to do something, somehow, and go back to Beirut to help his own people. But his boss would never let him go. Just the thought of asking for a leave of absence made him shudder. *My boss would fire me*! Naim would need to resign, but that would also mean the loss of his influence and income. What if ...

What if he could convince his boss, the wealthiest man in the Middle East, to endorse this project and fund it? The company does want to improve its public profile through corporate social responsibility. What if Naim timed it right and approach his boss when dining with his wife? That might work, as his wife had a calming effect on him. Still, Naim trembled at the thought of receiving his boss's wrath.

Would he take the risk? There was only one thing left he could do. Naim remembered his family's heritage. They had come from a long line of orthodox Christians, though he could not remember ever visiting a church before. Yet, the God of his forefathers was the God of heaven and earth, the Lord God Almighty, the defender of the widows and orphans. So Naim did what he had not done before; He kneeled and poured his heart out to his God and asked him for favor for what he was about to do: To ask his boss not only for time off, but also to fully fund his plan to rebuild the community in his homeland!

The following day, at a social event with all the corporate heads and spouses, Naim saw his opportunity. After a quick glance up to heaven, Naim took a bottle of the best wine over and filled the glasses of his boss and beautiful wife. They were in a good mood, but Naim had purposely put on a sad face. If they would notice, he had thought, they might ask why.

And it happened just so. The boss asked why Naim had such a sour face while partying. Had his latest girlfriend broken his heart? Naim quickly apologized and rattled off his experience watching the news the night before, and his desire to make a difference for his people, and his proposal to promote the company's social responsibility profile. To Naim's astonishment, his boss's reply was, "How much do you need and how long will it take?" Amazing! Truly amazing!

It's a Process

Naim's story is amazing, but it is both not true and true! It is not true because I made it up. However, it is true because it is based on the story of ... Nehemiah! (Did you guess?) Reading a modernized version of Nehemiah's story helps us appreciate how unique and remarkable it is.

What is also significant about Nehemiah's story is that it clearly outlines the process of city revitalization comparable to similar processes used by community development specialists today. City transformation is not an event, it is a process. As stated earlier in Chapter 2, Gornik outlined Nehemiah's city renovation project following the pattern of Wallace's theory for cultural revitalization. Gornik explains:

> By Wallace's account, revitalization is marked by six events: (1) the *mazeway [or worldview] reformulation*—usually that of an individual; (2) the *communication* of this vision to others, and their acceptance of it; (3) the *organization* of people around the goal of this vision; (4) the *adaptation* of the vision in response to resistance and in response to the patterns of the community; (5) wide acceptance of this new view of community, resulting in *cultural transformation;* and finally (6) the *routinization* of the transformative changes made.[105]

Gornik goes on to reframe the story of Nehemiah following Wallace's six stages, which can be outlined as shown in Table 2. For me as a pastor, this was a great outline for a sermon series, which I used to launch the Love Hanoi campaign (see Chapter 1, Love Hanoi: The Journey).[106] I highly recommend doing a series on Nehemiah for pastors who seek to launch a LOVE [YOUR CITY] initiative in their church.

Table 2: Nehemiah outline following Wallace's six stages of cultural revitalization[107]

Wallace's six stages	Nehemiah	Gornik's titles
1. **Reformulation**	1:1-10	Hearing a call
2. **Communication**	1:11-2:20	Beginning to take on the odds
3. **Organization**	3:1-32	A community becomes organized
4. **Adaptation**	4:1-7:4	Overcoming difficult obstacles
5. **Transformation**	7:5-10:39	New commitment to community
6. **Routinization**	11:1-13:31	Taking on new challenges

The rebuilding of Jerusalem's wall was a short-term 54-day project, a quick win, so to speak. This success created the buy-in and momentum needed for the true transformation which needed to take place in the hearts of the people and their leaders (Stages 4-5). We see that it is better to do a project to meet people's real felt needs first before trying to change their beliefs and behaviors.

THE MISSIONAL CYCLE

Our first Love Hanoi conference took place in 2013 at the local Hanoi Evangelical Church. Author and professor Johannes Reimer from Germany was our guest speaker. A wonderful storyteller with thousands of transformational testimonies up his sleeves, Reimer introduced the missional process to our little group of expats and Vietnamese listeners. One story particularly has stuck with me, which I have repeatedly retold since to illustrate the process of the missional cycle.

One church in Germany, after hearing Johannes speak and praying in response, decided to engage in a missional project to help a migrant community nearby. Johannes then visits the Imam of this Islamic community and poses this dilemma to him: "We have the same problem, you and I, because we both believe that we will be judged by God if we are not helping the poor. So why don't we help each other out and work together so we will not be judged?" The Imam agrees and they set out to run a soup kitchen for the migrants. Johannes returns to the church group and, together with them, develops a plan. Like any typical hardworking and efficient German, they reached the point of talking about the minute details. *How could they afford a vehicle for transporting food? Where could they get so many containers to store the food? Who would provide the food?* They were about to call it quits when Johannes said, "Don't worry about those things, I'll take care of these if you just organize the project and volunteers." They happily agreed!

Leaving the meeting, Johannes wondered how he could ever come up with those things: a large vehicle, thousands of containers, and lots of food. Coming home, he passes by his neighbor's house and sees a van parked in front which would be perfect for transportation. The neighbor comes out and asks Johannes, "Would you like this van? I'm trying to get rid of it. If you want, it's yours for free!" Still shocked by such instant provision, he walks into his home to find his wife talking with a guest. Johannes learns the man is a manufacturer of plasticware. When the guest hears Johannes' story, his response was, "How many thousands of containers do you need?"

Equipped with a mode of transportation and containers, the team can now collect expired food from the supermarkets in town for distribution at the migrant community. In the process, Johannes' relationship with the Imam turns into a friendship. They converse about their families, discuss each other's perspectives, and end up talking about their beliefs. One day, the Imam tells Johannes they have a problem: There is no food, and the people are counting on it. In response, Johannes prays to God for His provision, and when he finishes praying a truck pulls up. The driver asks, "Is this where I can offload my shipment of food? I accidentally came to the wrong village and my food will go bad, so they told me to come here!"

Later, the Imam asked Johannes, "Why is it that when I pray to Allah, nothing happens, but when you pray, God provides miraculously?" In due time, the Imam turned to faith in Isa (Jesus) and many in the community followed. As a result, a church of about 200 was established amidst this migrant settlement, unheard of in Germany and a large size by German standards!

This story illustrates the missional cycle, a community development process churches can implement to love their neighbors and see God's kingdom come and will be done in their communities. Not only do we need to change our posture towards the city, we also need to change the process, the way we approach the people we are trying to bless. The missional cycle will change the approach from coming with all the answers to asking the right questions.

As Johannes explained, people function at four levels: religious, intellectual, social, and material. What we believe influences what we think, which influences what we do and how we interact with other people, which then results in what we have. A person with skewed beliefs about herself may have a low self-esteem, ending up with the wrong friends and bad jobs, resulting in little material wealth. It is very hard to change people's beliefs, yet their beliefs need to be transformed to change their lives. However, starting at the top and working the way down is difficult. It is better to start from the bottom.

When we think of evangelism, too often Christians (and Evangelicals in particular) immediately think of having spiritual conversations with people about what we believe. We may not even be interested in listening first either! Starting conversations at the religious level is a difficult route to transforming lives. As we saw in the stories of Nehemiah and of the German migrant settlement, it is better to start ministry at the bottom level by meeting material needs. (If the person has no material needs, the next level of needs in family and interpersonal relationships may be the best way to start a ministry.) Working with the people and listening to them earns you the right to have a conversation about their life, family, and relationships. It is good practice to share family times together, open your home, and visit theirs. This builds trust and friendship, which opens discussions about what they think. Ideas, thoughts, and experiences can be shared. From there, it is just one step up to ask about their beliefs and to share about yours. This way, evangelism (sharing the good news) and extending the invitation to follow Jesus is a natural progression from service to acquaintance to friendship to fellowship. This is called the missional cycle (see Figure 18).

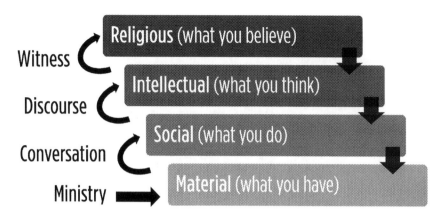

Figure 18: Four levels of society and the missional cycle[108]

The missional cycle uses this posture of service, listening, and relationship building to both do good and tell the good news. Jesus didn't just go around preaching, He also "went around doing good and healing all" (Acts 10:38). Often Jesus ministered to people's material need before sharing the good news of the kingdom's arrival. When Jesus helped people, *it was with no strings attached*, with unconditional love. Jesus' intention was to see them turn around and follow Him, but repentance was not a requirement for receiving His help. In the case of the ten lepers, only one of them returned, "and he was a Samaritan," Luke notes (17:16).

CHRISTIAN COMMUNITY DEVELOPMENT

Old Testament law and New Testament practice both had God's people engaged with the marginalized of society. "Religion that God our Father accepts as pure and faultless is this: to look after orphans and widows in their distress," stated Jesus' brother James (1:27). Widows, orphans, the poor, and immigrants were and still are of great concern to God. During the past century, community development has become a growing market across the globe. After World War II, European communities needed rebuilding and Christians were actively participating. In the USA, churches engaged in community development since the 1950s. Missionaries applied community development strategies among the unreached. Yet, with the ensuing dichotomy between sacred and secular, Evangelical churches lost touch with serving the common good of the communities in which they were placed. Thankfully, over the past two decades pioneers have paved the way of Christian Community Development (CCD).[109]

Like Wallace's six stages, community development follows a cycle of action steps that can be integrated with the missional cycle to create the cycle of CCD, to which I added the important step of Celebration (see Figure 19).

Figure 19: The cycle of CCD[110]

1. **Involvement:** First, a local church or Christian group needs to decide to get involved in their community. This can be geographic (i.e. their neighborhood, part of town, district, etc.), demographic (i.e. street children, forgotten elderly, drug addicts, etc.), or a combination of both. Like Nehemiah, it may happen that someone or a group is brokenhearted about the desperate situation in their community. This then becomes their calling.

2. **Context Analysis:** As Nehemiah inspected the walls, so must the context of the community and the issues be studied and analyzed. Prayer walking, information gathering, and street mapping are

common tools utilized to assess the neighborhood, learn its history, list the community's assets, and identify the real problem.

3. **Vision:** Although Scripture paints a picture of the ideal community, Christians should not assume that they have all the answers or that everyone is ready to listen. Nehemiah had a great testimony to share and a powerful vision for the city, yet he needed to transfer the ownership to the people who would be doing the work. That is the goal of the envisioning process, to create ownership.

4. **Concept:** Together with the people of the community, potential solutions and projects are identified. At the end of the brainstorming session, one project must be chosen for implementation. Priority must be given to what the residents or recipients view as most urgent and important. The key is to work together and not to impose outside ideas on the inside group. After a successful initial project, the community will be more open to outside ideas.

5. **Planning:** Nehemiah's wall project took a phenomenal amount of community organizing, including security details! It will be tempting to do projects *for* the community, but it is better to work *with* the people. Discovering their gifts, talents, and resources for use in the project is paramount to success.

6. **Action:** "So they began this good work," it's simply stated in Nehemiah 2:18. But then, don't forget to also have fun! This is where you rub shoulders with the people you seek to love and to help. During this period is where you earn trust, have conversations, build relationships, become personal, discuss issues, listen to their stories, and share your hopes and beliefs. The missional cycle takes place while in action, just like how Jesus shared his life and discipled his followers while on a mission.

7. **Evaluation:** Learning takes place during this stage. Formal and informal evaluation helps both the community and the Christian group to discover what went well and what could be better. This then informs the next project with the same community, or perhaps the same project but with another community.

8. **Celebration:** This is an important part at this stage. Just like Nehemiah held an enormous festival at the dedication of

the wall, so a block party or neighborhood festival will be a pivotal moment for the community. People can be thanked and recognized, testimonies and stories can be shared, success can be celebrated, and vision can be cast for what is next. It also may provide an opportunity for the Christian group to share about their motivations for their initial involvement, how they were transformed during the project, and what their hopes are for the community. This may create an opportunity for public sharing of the good news, which previously might not have been possible.

The CCD cycle can be repeated at the same locale, replicated in other communities by other churches, spread throughout the city, and end up in a citywide LOVE [YOUR CITY] festival. This has been the case in numerous cities around the world (San Diego, Hong Kong, Toronto, etc.) and a strategy the Luis Palau organization also employs.

ASSET BASED COMMUNITY DEVELOPMENT (ABCD)

In *To Live in Peace: Biblical Faith and the Changing Inner City,* Mark Gornik tells the story of how two families moved to Sandtown, a rundown Baltimore neighborhood, to start a church planting effort. They started with getting to know the neighbors and asking them about their dreams for Sandtown's future. "When the ability to dream a better future dies," Gornik says, "the consequences are life-destroying. We knew we needed to articulate our dreams for Sandtown."[111] With a few people gathered in his home on a Sunday morning, they raised the question, "What is God's dream for our community?"[112] Using a large sheet of newsprint paper and crayons, they started to draw images of what this new community would look like. Streets were renamed to "Hope" and "No Drugs," vacant lots disappeared, a church building with local architecture appeared, and church-run businesses and a community health center were drawn. None of the people present were professionals or experts, yet this initial visioning process was a powerful tool and a foundational piece to bringing those dreams into reality. Within 20 years, they established Sandtown Habitat for Humanity, New Song Community Church, New Song Community Learning Center, New Song Family Health Center, and the Eden Jobs and Economic Development program. Over 100 full-time staff worked for the various projects, 70% being original Sandtown residents. The Sandtown story is a prime example of a Christian asset-based community development project. The story started with the local residents, who together with young church planters drew their dreams with crayons on a blank piece of paper.

Asset Based Community Development (ABCD) seeks to mobilize the community to address its own agendas and challenges by answering the question: "What resources do we have to solve this problem ourselves?"[113] Rather than looking for outside help and resources right away, the community first looks internally to see how they can overcome the obstacles themselves with their own resources. Instead of being needs-driven, ABCD is capacity-focused. ABCD is a "glass half-full" approach, rather than a "half-empty" perspective. This approach not only makes a big difference for the practitioners, but especially for the residents themselves to be valued and seen for the strengths they have instead of the problems they face. The role of the community development practitioner is that of consultant, facilitator, and mobilizer, connecting people with one another, associations, corporations, institutions, and resources.[114]

Founders of the Asset Based Community Development Institute° in the USA John Kretzmann and John McKnight have authored several books and consulted the US government on community development. Kretzmann and McKnight were also Christians, which, although not explicitly stated in their resources, clearly shines through in their thinking. In fact, when reading their books, I frequently wondered if they were writing about church life or about community life. As it were, Kretzmann and McKnight have turned the church inside-out and applied principles of Christian community to the public sphere. ABCD is like doing church outside the four walls. If only every church would live inside-out and apply these principles both internally and externally, many communities would be in a much better place today!

The ABCD approach starts by mapping out the gifts and assets already present within the community, which are found at three levels: individuals, associations, and institutions. Figure 20 illustrates the various building blocks upon which the community can be built. The task of the practitioner

---

° For more details, visit www.abcdinstitute.org

is to discover the gifts of the individual residents through surveying the people within the community. Similar exercises are done with the leaders of associations and institutions. As this is quite an extensive project to implement within a neighborhood or a demographic group, a team of people is needed to gather, collect, and analyze the data. In the CCD cycle, this task would be accomplished during the Context Analysis stage.

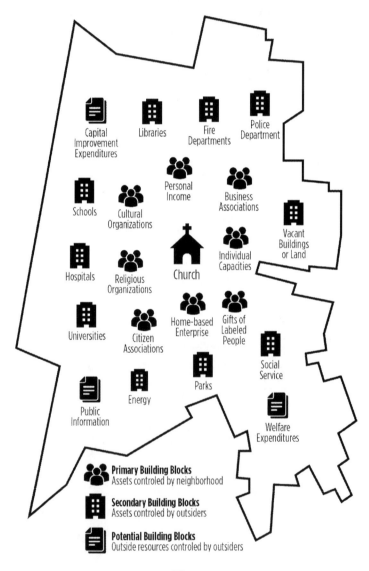

Figure 20: Community Asset Map[115]

Using local youth as an example, Kretzmann and McKnight identify the following assets we otherwise might not consider as a resource for community development: time, ideas, creativity, connection to place, dreams, desires, peer and family relationships, peer role models, enthusiasm, and energy.[116] The next step is to connect the recipients with potential partners in the community such as public institutions, private corporations, civic associations, and individual residents (see Figure 21). The result can create an astounding network map of one-on-one relationships between the recipients and the partners (see Figure 22). This exercise can be done for any demographic grouping within a community, such as the elderly, disabled, unemployed, drug addicts, street children, local artists, etc.

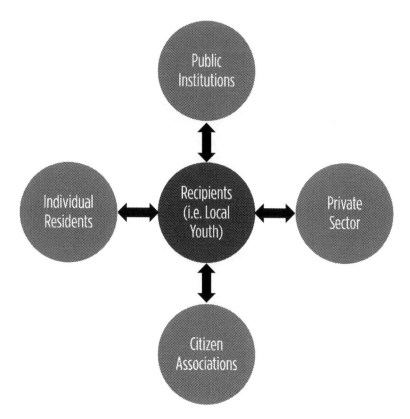

Figure 21: Potential Partners[117]

Figure 22: One-on-one relationships between recipients and partners[118]

As discussed under Posture, church leaders have a difficult time not seeing their church at the center, but as a part of the local associations. It is important that the community knows churches can be a resource, a help, a pool of volunteers, a facility available for community activities, etc. The same mapping strategy can be used to develop a one-on-one relationship network between the church and the community (see Figure 23). To be clear, the initial posture is to be a blessing to the community, not to seek the church's self-interest. However, in the process churches may also find themselves being on the receiving end of their neighbor's generosity and free will.

Figure 23: One-on-one relationships between local church and the community for mutual benefit[119]

Kretzmann and McKnight list a number of ideas based on actual experiences of how local churches can contribute to the rebuilding of their community's economy.[120] These are:

- Establish a foundation through which investment or grants are made in neighborhood-based projects
- Publish a newsletter which promotes minority-owned businesses
- Create an employment opportunity program and provide labor support through local contracts
- Allow local business associations to use the facility, promoting local business code of ethics and fair hiring practices

- Form a community credit union with other partners to invest in community-based projects
- Lease a gas station for the local community
- Set up a church-based loan pool for community outreach

With the ABCD approach, the emphasis is on identifying local assets and leveraging those to build the community. The local community can utilize outside resources, but only "to support a locally driven development," state Kretzmann and McKnight. "[O]nly when a broadly representative group of citizens have begun to solve problems together, and to hammer out a shared vision and set of strategies—*only then* should the community begin to consider leveraging resources from the outside."[121]

In *Walking with the Poor,* Myers challenges us to question what we mean with *transformation.* We must ask ourselves "what we believe people are being transformed *from* and transformed *to.*"[122] It is a Western myth that human progress in the forms of capitalism, globalization, science, and technology will save the poor. We (western practitioners and missionaries) often come with our preconceived ideas, even our "Christian" ideas, of what a better future looks like for the poor. We come in, assess the problems, provide solutions, and perhaps never ask the poor person what changes they would like to see and how. The poor are survivors and innovators, with local knowledge and a rich history. They may not want a wireless laptop computer but just some pen and paper. It is far better to sit down together, ask the right questions, and start drawing a picture of what a better future looks like. As Myers states,

> The poor must come to believe in themselves—not in us, our development aid, or our development agency. If they believe we are the true instruments of development, then we have failed to create mental sustainability. Instead, we have created dependency and deepened their poverty.[123]

When thinking of assets, we often think primarily about financial capital or material possessions. Assets, however, can be any kind of resource a person or community has that can be built upon for their betterment.

In the marketplace, we have come to consider employees as human capital and properties as physical capital. We can continue this line of thought and look at social capital, environmental capital, political capital, and cultural capital as assets of a community. Here are seven assets with a brief description based on *Asset Building & Community Development* by Gary Paul Green and Anna Haines:

1. **Human Capital:** This includes "general education background, labor market experience, artistic development and appreciation, health, and other skills and experience."[124] Communities and Community Based Organizations (CBOs) often engage in workforce development through training, recruitment, placement, mentoring, and follow-up. The CBO functions like a hub, aligning the labor supply with demand, often networking with businesses, government, educational institutions, and other non-profits. Offering vocational skills training, English language clubs, micro- and small enterprise development, workforce development, capacity building, and matching workers with job opportunities are all worthwhile ideas.

2. **Social Capital:** Relationships are foundational to community building and organizing. "Social relationships and networks serve as a form of capital because they require investments in time and energy, with the anticipation that individuals can tap into these resources when necessary. ... These resources are referred to as social capital."[125] Community centers, public spaces, and city architecture can encourage the building of such relationships. CBOs can facilitate public gatherings and debate, such as the visioning meeting described earlier, as well as diversity in leadership.

3. **Physical Capital:** "Sense of a place is shaped by the local physical capital: its roads, buildings (houses, businesses, [retail stores], warehouses), and other physical features (railroad tracks, bridges, [water, sewers], vacant land)."[126] Housing is one of the major components of community development, addressing issues such as affordability, adequacy, availability, and accessibility.

Homelessness is an issue in Hanoi, although it is not clear where the homeless find a place to sleep. Street children were recently reported to be sleeping on top of the pillars underneath the Long Bien Bridge, about 30 meters above the surface! CBOs and NGOs will need to have a good understanding of the local housing market and regulations.

4. **Financial Capital**: "Many poor and minority communities are creating alternative credit institutions (e.g., community development credit unions, community development banks, revolving loan funds, and microenterprise loan funds) to address their credit needs."[127] The poor generally lack access to financial capital, thus many NGOs provide micro- and small loans for business development or help communities set up revolving loan funds. HIF contributed to such a fund for a working group of women with HIV/AIDS through World Concern, a Christian Non-Government Organization (NGO).

5. **Environmental Capital:** This includes "several aspects of a community's base of natural resources: air, water, land, flora, and fauna."[128] Natural resources are important because of the risks posed to the community, such as floods, pollution, and waste, and benefits like recreation, beauty, or heritage. Urban sprawl is a common issue in most cities, though in developing nations these often result in slum areas. Lack of proper sewage, clean water, and sanitation is a huge issue in shantytowns. Can Christians in Hanoi see themselves involved in environmental organizations as stewards of God's creation and architects of places rich in nature? Air, noise, and light pollution are huge issues in the city—can we do something about it? Can we help plant more trees and create urban gardens?

6. **Political Capital:** Max Weber, the German philosopher, "defined power broadly as the ability to influence others despite resistance. ... Power is at the heart of political capital." Community power structures can be analyzed through three methods: "reputational, positional, and decision making."[129] The first is to discover what people carry influence in the community.

The second is to identify who hold the positions of power. The third is to examine the community's history to find out who the winners were when critical decisions needed to be made. Working with the local power structures and learning how to gain access to political power is essential in community development. One caveat, however, is that local powers may not appreciate others gaining more influence than what they have.

7. **Cultural Capital:** "[A] community's cultural resources, such as historic buildings, archaeological sites, museums, farmers' markets, and ethnic festivals, in many ways define and bring identity to a community. Unfortunately, cultural resources are often viewed as something consumed by the rich and not related to middle-class and working-class residents."[130] Arts, music, dance, architecture, and festivals are often overlooked in community development work.

So, you (and/or your church) have decided to get involved in your community or a specific demographic, segment or target group of a community. You also have analyzed the context, issues, and opportunities. Backed by Scripture, you have a vision for how that community can become more reflective of God's kingdom and be transformed by shalom. You have met with the community leaders or residents and are ready to start with a project. As you do not want to rely on outside resources, but build on local assets, what are some potential concepts for projects that you can start with? Something small and short to build relationships, gain trust, test the collaboration, and experience a quick win would be great. That is what *Seed Projects* are especially good for: initial initiatives that can be repeated as needed and desired.

SEED PROJECTS

In Hanoi, seed projects are very popular among local churches because they are small and can be done independently to bless the local community. Special occasions such as Children's Day, Mid-Autumn Festival, Christmas, and Tet holiday are especially favored because these are festive times during which communities already organize events (except for Christmas, but this is becoming hugely popular). Churches like to give gifts or support for the poor, children, students, disabled, patients, or veterans. These are one-time or annual events and generate goodwill with community leaders and citizens. Some churches have held free medical checkups, given free haircuts, or donated free wheelchairs.

Seeds are one of the word pictures Jesus used in Scripture, and they have great implications for service. Jesus said, "I tell you the truth, unless a kernel of wheat falls to the ground and dies, it remains only a single seed. But if it dies, it produces many seeds" (John 12:24). Seeds illustrate sacrifice. They die to do what they were created to do—produce fruit. They are small, but when they die, they yield great multiplication.

Jesus reminded us that the impact of our service is not something for which we can take credit: "I sent you to reap what you have not worked for. Others have done the hard work, and you have reaped the benefits of their labor" (John 4:38). God is already at work in the hearts of those to whom we minister. Whenever there is an impact for the kingdom, the credit belongs to God, not to us.

The apostle Paul wrote: "So neither he who plants nor he who waters is anything, but only God, who makes things grow. The man who plants and the man who waters have one purpose, and each will be rewarded according to his own labor" (1 Corinthians 3:7-8). The purpose of our service is the expansion of Christ's reign—the will of God, done on earth as it is in heaven. The objective is the extension of the kingdom, not numerical church growth, which is a side-product.

A seed project is small, short-term ministry by a local church. It is done with local resources to demonstrate God's love to those outside the faith community. The purpose of a seed project is to use a simple, effective, and proven tool to help a local church to begin to demonstrate God's love to people outside of the Body of Christ; and to enable local churches to be proclaimers of the gospel in deed.

Moffit, in *Seeds and Seed Projects, explains the* key benefits to deploying seed projects:[P]

[P]   Adapted from Bob Moffit, "Seeds and Seed Projects," (2007). For more information, visit www.harvestfoundation.org and www.disciplenations.org.

- Seed projects enable the churches that practice them to see the power that the simple and consistent demonstration of God's love has in drawing people into the Kingdom.
- Seed projects help grassroots churches see that God uses small, locally resourced activities in powerful, lasting ways.
- Seed projects build experience and confidence for much larger activities.

Seed projects are motivated by God's intentions for the community and must be covered in prayer. Although they are small and short, they need to be well planned. As much as possible, local resources should be used, with outside resources used only in addition after people have demonstrated willingness to sacrificially use their own resources. Seed projects do not manipulate; they should reflect God's heart of compassion for the brokenness of people's lives. Seed projects are directed toward those outside the church and those who benefit should also participate as much as possible.

For seed projects to have their maximum impact, they should be well-balanced, focused, and ongoing. Demonstrations of love should not be something that happen only once or twice a year. God's love should be a part of the continuous ministry and way of life for individual Christians and for their churches over a long period. At the end, the seed project is for the glory of God and for people to experience God's love in tangible ways. As Jesus said, "Let your light shine before others, that they may see your good deeds and glorify your Father in heaven" (Matthew 5:16).

In 2019, through the Love in Action network, 16 churches organized a variety of projects on the occasion of Children's Day on June 1. Each church sent representatives for the two-day Seed Project training, designed their own project, and implemented it with their own resources, which was matched up to $500/church by a donor. This effort was well received by all the community leaders, creating positive relationships between churches and local governments.

Below are listed 40 different seed projects already being done by churches in Hanoi and around the world. Some are very small and simple while others take more resources and time. Most projects use local manpower and resources and can be done in partnership with other churches and organizations. These seed project ideas can be replicated but should not stop you from designing your own seed projects in collaboration with their communities.[q]

1. **Blood drive:** Recruit people to go to a clinic or to host a clinic for donating blood, invite other churches, organizations, neighbors

2. **Care for children:** Find out first the needs of children in your community, not presuming the perceived need is correct

3. **Medical checkups:** Host a free clinic in your church facility, or go out as a team to the target community, together with a nurse, doctor and/or dentist

4. **Student scholarships:** Offer a scholarship program for underprivileged children regardless of their status or beliefs

5. **English clubs:** Helping people practice English is helpful everywhere, even in English-speaking countries, for students, migrants, and professionals. HIF utilizes Spotlight English Clubs, which does not require teaching skills, and is values-based on Christian principles[r]

6. **Soft skills training:** Coaching, cooking, organizing, career planning, dance, art, car repair, accounting, you name it, anyone can teach someone their skill (asset) by doing things together

7. **Cleanup street/park:** Grab some extra long cooking tongs or trash pickup tool, an extra heavy garbage bag, work gloves, and plenty of water, and hit the streets and parks and lakeshores and beaches to clean them up with a small group (your church cell group) or a large collaborative group (HIF joined a group cleaning 14 tons by 140 people in two days!)

8. **Garbage to garden:** Is garbage collecting on a street corner? Work with the local community to turn it into a garden area. Sometimes just putting some plants there will do the job!

---

[q] Seed projects listed from numbers 9 to 39 are adapted from Reimer, "Community Transformation, Peace and Church Growth."

[r] Visit www.spotlightenglish.com for more information

9. **Walk path for blind:** Especially in developing nations, navigating sidewalks (if they exist) can be treacherous for the blind. Why not at least fix a section to make a path for the blind?

10. **Clean public toilets:** Ugh, right?! But someone's gotta do it and your church could set the tone (and change the smell!)

11. **Streetlights:** Sponsor or install lights in dark corners of the city, especially if acts of violence are known to happen in these areas

12. **Employment agency:** Let professionals in your church set up an employment broker for the destitute, new graduates, veterans, retirees, parolees, recovering addicts, etc. in need of work

13. **Jobs for disabled:** Intentionally work on capacity building and job placement for the disabled, providing ongoing support while at work

14. **Help a neighbor:** Offer to do simple chores like mowing lawns, washing windows, buying groceries, shoveling snow, repairing vehicles, babysitting, helping with the computer, etc. This can be done as an event, a Love Your City week, or an ongoing effort

15. **Before/after school care:** Many cannot afford daycare before or after work, yet churches often have space and people with time. A church in Hanoi hosts children after school while they wait for parents to pick them up and eventually the kids want to come on Sundays too, bringing family!

16. **Kindergarten:** Does your church have classrooms? This is an excellent asset to turn into a daycare or kindergarten!

17. **Lease grandparents:** In cities, generations are often divided, longing for one another. Grandparents can be "leased" to families without grandparents nearby

18. **Visit the sick:** At hospitals, clinics, those stuck at home, bedridden, the old and young, you are visiting Jesus in disguise!

19. **Comfort the dying:** People can feel lonely at the end of life, especially if friends and family have distanced themselves or have passed away already

20. **Chaplaincy:** A chaplain is like a pastor and first responder combined who work outside the walls of the church. Training and certification can be obtained (the International Fellowship of

Chaplains[s] now provides training in Hanoi) and your church can offer this asset to your community or city to meet real felt needs in times of crisis

21. **Help the homeless:** Providing shelter and long-term housing is a great starting point to help those without homes, as well as linking them with other agencies. Randomly giving out food and clothing may be less helpful or even hurting their situation

22. **Community center:** Become a center for your community and utilize your space to offer and host community events, classes, clubs, etc.

23. **Marriage enrichment:** Provide a romantic date night for couples while taking them through a marriage course or class. The creators of the Alpha Course offer a pre-marriage and marriage course to do just that![t]

24. **Parental training class:** No degree is needed to become a parent, but most would love more input from respected leaders or quality courses. Alpha also offers Parenting Children and Parenting Teens courses[u]

25. **Money management:** Helpful for all, but especially for teens, students, midlife retirement planning, social entrepreneurs, and particularly for the economically poor (micro-finance schemes are highly successful)

26. **Gardening club:** Be an initiator of a community garden, even if on rooftops! Urban gardening and locally grown vegetables are becoming greatly popular

27. **Bicycle riding/repair shop:** Riding a bicycle may not be a skill migrant students or workers have learned, or could afford, but offers a way to build relationships and offer a practical service

28. **Used clothing fair:** A popular activity among Western churches, this can be practiced around the world to collect clothing for

---

[s] Visit www.ifoc.org for more information

[t] Visit www.themarriagecourses.org for more information

[u] Find out more at www.themarriagecourses.org/try-parenting/the-parenting -children-course

donation or to organize a large yard/garage sale to raise funds for charity

29. **Wedding team:** To help those who cannot afford weddings, or as an outreach to those preferring a "Western" or "church" wedding, which could include premarital counseling or courses

30. **Funeral team:** Depending on the surrounding context and if Christian practice is similar, a team could help those without resources or family with funeral organization

31. **Home repair team:** Helping those in need with their home repairs like the church in downtown Hanoi is doing for the elderly who are forsaken by their children

32. **Learning/literacy/language program:** Offering help to those with learning disabilities or from disadvantaged backgrounds, those needing to learn reading and writing, and those wanting to learn the host language or another language (international churches often have 50 or more language groups represented, a big asset for the community!)

33. **College preparation:** Assisting students to get ready for college (if not offered at school), while having these students in return help younger children with homework

34. **Job application:** Assisting college grads, the unemployed, disadvantaged, and others in applying for jobs, interviews, resume writing, etc.

35. **Marriage and family counseling:** A more intense process requiring greater skills, although this can be started by mature members mentoring younger couples. HIF helped start a counseling center to serve the international and local community in Hanoi in this area of need

36. **Conflict mediation:** For years Johannes Reimer asked taxi drivers at airports around the world to take them to a place where people resolve conflict, but only once was he brought to a church! Your church can be the first in your city as a place of peace and reconciliation

37. **Playgrounds for young and old:** The Lord showed through Zechariah (8:4-6) that He values both the young and old being

able to enjoy spending time outside. By providing public space, the church can engage with their community

38. **Arts and sports facility:** Multi-purpose church facilities can be offered for arts, dance, and sports recreation, serving people who otherwise would not step inside a church building

39. **Government relations:** Political leaders and government workers can benefit from spiritual advice, encouragement, or recognition. In Africa, one church held a festival to celebrate, thank, and recognize law enforcement, improving their relationship immediately

40. **Your project:** What would you add to this list? No idea is too crazy for God!

Loving your city and getting involved in the community to bring revitalization is a process. Rather than first trying to change what people believe, the Christian Community Development process starts at the level of people's felt material needs. This is where we can most practically express the love of Christ in tangible ways, not unlike Jesus Himself. Working with people rather than doing things for them is the way to go about it, building on their assets instead of relying on outside resources. Seed projects are a great way to get started and see quick results, which encourages the community and the partnership to move to the next level of engagement. What then is a partnership and how do they differ from networks? How can partnerships bridge boundaries in society and across religious lines? What should you pay attention to when partnering cross-culturally and working with an ethnically diverse team? Move on over to Step 4: Partner.

CHAPTER 7

PARTNER

"I in them and you in me, that they may become
perfectly one, so that the world may know that you
sent me and loved them even as you loved me."

John 17:23

"The risk was unacceptable!," the pediatrician said as we discussed the Long Bien cleanup project in hindsight. "The bacterial infections from that sewer water could have seriously harmed someone," he insisted, and I couldn't have agreed more. I had heard that a doctor had been sent by one of the schools to make sure that none of their students would be at risk and that he had been quite upset with the lack of hygiene and apparent recklessness of the organizers to expose volunteers to such health risks. Yet, we had and still we did an amazing work!

Keep Hanoi Clean is an initiative started by an American young man who'd been teaching English in Hanoi, like so many other young adults like him. However, as he fell in love with the city, James Kendall could no longer stand the heaps of trash spoiling Hanoi's charm. In 2016, James decided to take matters in his own hands and started cleaning up streets, parks and canals (although they were more like sewers!). Hanoians were amazed, stunned, impressed, upset, thankful, and inspired. Some started joining him and Keep Hanoi Clean (KHC) was born.

A year later, during one of the cleanup days, I joined James and his crew of volunteers who had responded to the media post that day. We had lunch together and I discovered that in the process we were building community among the group. We talked while picking up trash and enjoyed vegan food while hunched on plastic chairs by the lakeside. Once

I started promoting KHC at HIF, our youth got involved and other adults joined as well. James attended one of our Love Hanoi conferences and loved it! Then, during the lead up to the Festival, James asked HIF's help to clean up a seriously trashed and neglected corner at the bottom of Long Bien bridge on the edge of a migrant community.

We were stunned, to say the least! The looks on people's faces when we arrived on site told it all: There's no way we can clean this mess! A "creek" of sewage water streamed down to the Red River along the bridge's foundation, with layers and layers of trash on both banks. Garbage collection had not been arranged by the city for this neighborhood, so the trash had just accumulated over the years, as evidenced by the pungent odor. The pediatrician was right in saying that it didn't look safe, but we were all adults and decided to have a go at it. KHC had made the arrangements with the ward's political leaders and rallied up a large crew of volunteers, while HIF had recruited local churches to join and help.

It took 140 people to clean out 14 tons of trash over one weekend! Hanoi TV came out to record and report the event on the local news. Although it would have been better if the community's residents had also participated (as described in the ABCD process), this project became a great example of collaboration between churches, a non-Christian charity group, local government, the waste management company, and local media. When you love your city and seek the shalom of the city to the benefit of the people, it is possible to partner across all kinds of boundaries: societal, cultural, geographical, political, organizational, and denominational.

"Let us start rebuilding," the people had replied to Nehemiah (2:18), and they worked shoulder-to-shoulder until the wall was done. We also can (re)build our cities together with our fellow citizens next to us, regardless of their position in life. In addition, the process provides a great opportunity for building community together! In this chapter, I will explore the meaning and practice of partnerships, how partnering differentiates from networking, and how partnering across boundaries can be done more effectively.

PARTNERSHIP

"Too big to do alone and too important not to do together!" This was the slogan of the Missio Nexus conference in 2018, which focused on partnership,[v] and describes our motivation to collaborate within the Body of Christ and across boundaries. Not only do Christians need to work together for the gospel's sake, but Christians also need to work together with non-Christians for the kingdom's sake. As Swanson and Williams put it, the church needs to become "a visible, united presence that seeks the city's good."[131] It is then that the church positions itself as a willing partner to collaborate for the benefit of the city and for the glory of our heavenly Father.

Partnership among Christians is "a complementary relationship driven by a common purpose and sustained by a willingness to learn and grow together in obedience to God," says Daniel Rickett. Within a healthy partnership, the partners help "to build one another's capacity" and work towards "mutual development."[132] Jesus prayed for the unity of the church so that "the world will know that you sent me and have loved them" (John 17:23). Unity does not mean "uniformity of doctrine, uniformity of programming, or uniformity in the way we pray or worship," state Swanson and Williams. As the apostle Paul points out, the church is one unit already, namely the body of Christ with its various diverse parts. These parts just need to work together, rather than seeing themselves as separate, superior, or inferior. The church can find unity in mission. A common external goal, namely loving the city for the Father's glory, can work wonders in developing unity among the city's churches.

One success story of this kind of unity is the story of Unite!, a partnership of churches in the region of Atlanta, Georgia. Founder and director Chip Sweney tells the story of Unite! in *A New Kind of Big: How Churches of Any Size Can Partner to Transform Communities*.[133] An initiative of Perimeter Church, Sweney researched "the 12-mile radius around our church to discover the needs and to find the groups already meeting those needs." The church then established partnerships with local institutions already providing community services, rather than starting

---

[v] Learn more about Missio Nexus at www.missionexus.org

their own projects and programs. A volunteer weekend was organized to connect church members with these local partners, which turned out to be a huge success. Volunteers not only served that weekend, but also continued to work with the local partners.

What started as one church's volunteer weekend in 2007 grew into a regional network of more than 200 churches collaborating together for community transformation. "Big is important because God is bigger and because the need is big," writes Sweney. "The issues—like injustice and poverty and hunger—are bigger than any one person can address. Our cities and countries and continents are bigger than any one church can influence."[134]

Tom Mullins, a former colleague of Sweney, explained to me that when Hurricane Katrina hit the region in 2005, the city's government called Unite! for their help with coordinating relief efforts because they were the only network that was so well connected across the city! In the past, Perimeter Church had been internally focused and if it had disappeared, no one outside the church would have cared, Tom told me. As a direct result of forming Unite!, the church now stands united with other churches through the city and is integral to the city's welfare. In a personal interview, Sweney stated that over time Unite! had become "an incubator for partnerships," and that "even some non-profits have come into existence through the partnerships."[135] This is exactly the next point I would like to make, the role of networking in fostering partnerships.

NETWORKING

Understanding the difference between networks and partnerships was very helpful to me in the process of developing the Love Hanoi campaign. Phill Butler, who might be considered the father of partnership and networking in the global world of Christian mission, sheds light on this matter. In his book, *Well Connected,*[w] he differentiates networks and partnerships in a simple but profound way:

---

[w] Download the book for free in English and other languages at www.visionsynergy. net/tools-and-training

Networks:

"Any group of individuals or organizations, sharing a common interest, who regularly communicate with each other *to enhance their individual purposes.*"

Partnerships:

"Any group of individuals or organizations, sharing a common interest, who regularly communicate, *plan and work together to achieve a common vision beyond the capacity of any one of the individual partners.*"

Both networks and partnerships consist of a group of individuals or organizations who share a common interest and who regularly communicate with each other. The difference is in the goal: a network exists to "enhance their individual purposes," while a partnership aims to "work together to achieve a common vision beyond the capacity of any one of individual partners." I have found that partnerships cannot be forced upon people, pastors, churches or organizations. We cannot make people partner together, but we can inspire, stimulate, and create environments to facilitate the germination of partnerships through networking. As Butler stated and Sweney echoed, networks "are incubators for partnerships."[136]

The City Ministry Network Model by Butler is a helpful model to illustrate how networking facilitates the flow of resources through partnerships to urban ministry projects (see Figure 24). For example, at HIF we have established CityPartners as our local outreach ministry. Through CityPartners (CP), we seek to create partnerships so that everyone in the city can flourish. Our aim is to *inspire* people to love the least, the last and the lost; to *network* local and international partners; and to *connect* resources with opportunities to give and to serve. In so doing, we hope to bring about transformational and sustainable change in Hanoi. In the following diagram, the CityPartners logo could be placed in the center of the ministry network oval and it would perfectly explain what CP is trying to accomplish.

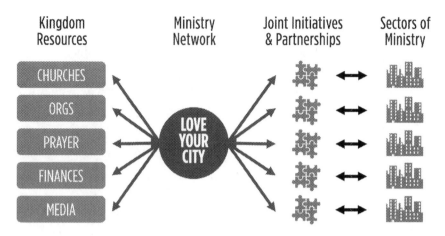

Figure 24: City Ministry Network Model[137]

In the next chapter I will go into detail about different ways to gather and network people. Furthermore, I will be talking about the staging of Love Hanoi conferences, which has yielded fruits for us in terms of partnerships.

One example of a partnership outcome from the first Love Hanoi conference is the story of one of the diplomats in HIF, a Police Attaché to his embassy in Hanoi. One of his tasks is to prevent illegal human trafficking from Asia to his country. Having heard the presentation of ColorMe, a new anti-trafficking initiative formed by HIF and a local drug rehab, he was inspired to organize a roundtable meeting with other Christian organizations, non-Christian organizations, and government and diplomatic institutions, who are focused on human trafficking prevention. This was hosted by CityPartners at HIF and resulted in a new network being born. Today, the diplomat has over 1,000 contacts on his phone to warn any port authority or agent in the SE Asia region of potential trafficking and can stop it from happening by a text message over social media apps. It is amazing what kind of partnerships and outcomes can result from providing a platform and an environment that fosters partnerships to form.

CITYWIDE NETWORKS

One unique feature of what God is doing in cities around the world is uniting churches to form citywide networks to seek the shalom of the city, to pray for it, and to do good deeds, all for the Father's glory. Love Boulder inspired Love Hanoi and numerous other citywide networks as a result of Swanson and William's work. Unite! in Atlanta was one result of that, which in turn inspired For Charlotte in North Carolina, and probably many others who read Sweney's book. Although CityPartners is a network in Hanoi, it is only HIF's outreach ministry. Therefore, we saw the need for a new citywide network to be established that would unite pastors and ministry leaders with a heart for the city and their communities. As the tide of the Love Hanoi Festival raised all ships, it provided an opportune time to launch the Love in Action network to do just that in Hanoi.

In Vietnamese, the translation is literally "Love Equals Action." It is a fine interpretation of what Love Hanoi and Love [Your City] is all about. Not loving with just words, but loving our city, communities, and neighbors with action. This counteracts a mindset that exists among many Vietnamese church leaders (and likely across the world) that church resources (money and people) should not be used for non-church activities outside their church. If the activity does not benefit their church directly (i.e. church growth through evangelism) then why invest resources in it? This challenge provides a double barrier: Why partner with other churches if the effort does not directly benefit my church and potentially may benefit someone else's church more? Why partner across church boundaries if the effort benefits people outside the church, i.e. non-Christian people in the community and the city? Especially if the church cannot evangelize the beneficiaries at the event or through the project, then why bother at all?

This brings us back to the first step, Principles, where church leaders and members need a biblical understanding of our mandate to be stewards of all creation, love our neighbors unconditionally, and do good to those in need because this is how we emulate and serve Jesus. As Paul wrote to the Philippian church, *have the same mindset as Christ Jesus: Who, being in very nature God, did not consider equality with God something to be used to his own advantage; rather, he made himself nothing by taking the very nature of a servant.* (Philippians 2:5-7)

Jesus' integrity was 100% pure and perfect, He did not treat a Jew differently than a non-Jew. We can read accounts of Him doing loving acts for people regardless of their race, gender, age, or status; whether they were considered "in" or "out." In fact, He preferred to search out, hang out with, and go out of His way for those who were the least, the last, and the lost: the Samaritan woman at the well five times divorced, the blind beggar calling His name along the road, the leper shouting "unclean" while walking through town, the children who were pushed aside by adults, the man born blind who was kicked out of the temple for being healed, and on and on the stories go. Jesus invested a great deal of His resources on those "outside" the "church" of His day. It is this mission and passion that unites us to seek the shalom of the city, to present a united front, to demonstrate that God so loved the world that He sent His only Son.

CROSS-SECTOR COLLABORATION

The city is too big for just one group, or even two, to reach. One effective way to minister to the whole city is by breaking it down into more sizeable segments (although still huge) or also known as the concept of domains. Popularized as the "Seven Mountains" by Loren Cunningham (founder of YWAM) and Bill Bright (founder of Campus Crusade for Christ), they talked of the seven spheres of influence in society: Family, God's People (church), Education, Media, Culture, Economy (science, tech, production, business), and Government (judicial, legislative, and executive).[138]

Using the story of Caleb who at old age said, "Give me this mountain," Cunningham and Bright viewed each sphere of society as a mountain to climb by Christians wanting to see God's kingdom come and will be done in their sector of work. This way, every believer can be equipped for mission in their sphere, sector, industry, or domain, however it may be called: plumbers, CEOs, pilots, nurses, waiters, counselors, artists, scientists, teachers, and you name it—God's mission is for every believer, not just pastors and missionaries! They could serve God in their jobs locally at home or go globally into regions where professional ministry leaders are less welcome.

Bob Roberts calls this concept "glocal church." In his book, *Glocalization: How followers of Jesus engage a flat world,* Bob writes:

> When the church glocalizes, it acts as a connection center between believers and all of society's domains. It focuses on training the people in the pew how to view their vocation as the "Jerusalem" in terms of ministry. From there it motivates them toward how they can use that vocation to intersect a domain locally—and globally—throughout the ends of the earth! The church connects to society through the natural infrastructures, equipping and sending people through their jobs to affect a particular domain.[139]

Like the earlier illustration used in the chapter on Posture (see Figure 15), a domain model may look like a segmented pie chart with each of the domains grouped by the three sectors of society: public, private, and non-profit. Or it could look like a bubble chart, like Roberts used. During a conversation with Bob Roberts, he told me his "secret" about choosing these domains: he used the jobs opportunities page in the newspaper and used those headlines! There is nothing holy or sacred about the "Seven Mountains," spheres, domains, or sectors. It is best to contextualize them for your city and society (and have fun with the charts!). In Hanoi, we use the domains chart frequently in HIF and with Love in Action (see Figure 25). Once every year or so we group our church members by domains after service to meet one another and form connections, decide whether to create a prayer group or initiative for their sphere of work. Often the results are more focused on discovering who else works in the same domain, but sometimes a prayer group or initiative comes out of it. This certainly can be leveraged to a greater extent.

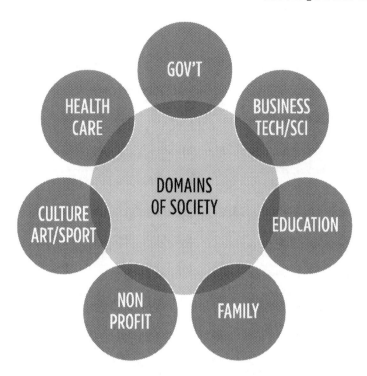

Figure 25: Domains of Society as used by HIF

Citywide, the churches have done and are doing numerous initiatives, projects, and events on an individual basis for their communities, which can be grouped together by domain to get a broader perspective. Here is a list of sample activities currently done by churches and Christians:

Healthcare:
- Hold blood drives
- Community health education
- Run Christian clinics
- Host free medical checkups

Education:
- Provide scholarships
- Tutor students
- Teach English
- Establish private schools

Family:
- Train in parent-coaching
- Counsel married couples
- Run parenting courses
- Provide afterschool care

Culture:
- Organize football leagues
- Hold arts exhibitions
- Organize joint concerts
- Perform worship dance

Business:
- Train family businesses
- Mentor college graduates
- Establish social enterprises
- Create workplace videos

Non-profit:
- Rehabilitate drug addicts
- Support the disabled
- Foster children
- Help the poor

Governance:
- Hold roundtable forums
- Visit during holidays
- Clean neighborhoods
- Provide disaster relief

I was pleasantly surprised when I compiled my research data on the current level of engagement by churches in their communities for my doctoral thesis. Churches and Christians in Hanoi are already active with so many activities in each domain! But what if, instead of just thinking and doing seed projects, we could understand and tackle citywide issues of each domain? Blood drives will not solve all the healthcare issues in Hanoi. Cleaning streets will not tackle the daunting environmental challenges of the city. Scholarships will not transform the educational system that is behind international standards. We as the Church in Hanoi need to be able to think and act citywide to really contribute to the shalom of the city and society. If Christians across cities around the globe would collaborate across boundaries in such a way, the world would be a better place for everyone, especially for those at the bottom of society!

Networking and partnering by domains at a citywide level is more challenging but has far greater potential. For the Love in Action network, this will be the next step, to develop a citywide vision for each domain and potential action steps at macro and micro scale. The plan is to form a working group for each domain and implement the following steps:

1. Research the **facts**, statistics, current issues
2. Develop a **theology** for each domain[x]

---

[x] Landa Cope has done a fabulous job developing a theology for each domain in her book, *Old Testament Template*. Find out more at www.templateinstitute.com.

3. Discover the current **practice** of churches and Christians
4. Create a **vision** of what could be based on theology
5. Identify the **opportunities** for churches to engage in

At the end of this process, the results will be compiled into a report that can be distributed widely, as well as posted on the Love in Action website. This exercise will create many opportunities for Christians to work together across church, denominational, and vocational boundaries as they meet and collaborate with believers in their domain of work from other congregations. The outcome will be that suddenly everyone will be able to learn and have the same knowledge.

Right now, I am not aware of any Christian in Hanoi who knows something about every domain. There is no collective knowledge, everyone knows about what they are doing, but no one has a citywide perspective. However, at the end of this process, everyone will know the same thing everyone else knows, providing a broad base of shared learning and knowledge upon which to build the citywide network and future partnerships. Church leaders and Christians will be able to understand how they can be engaged in each domain at a citywide level to tackle the urban issues collaboratively across boundaries, while at the same time develop strategies and seed projects to be implemented by their church at the local community level. For that to be successful, a better understanding of partnering across boundaries is needed.

PARTNERING ACROSS BOUNDARIES

It takes a unique kind of leader to provide the leadership needed for a cross-organizational, cross-denominational, cross-sectoral, and cross-cultural collaboration. In *Leading Across Boundaries,* Linden uses the concept of "court vision" from basketball, when "a player looks at one spot on the court but can see what's happening in a 180-degree arc."

People who collaborate well also have good court vision. Like successful basketball players and other team athletes, they communicate laterally, look for ways to share ideas, and form relationships well. They tend to be natural networkers, understanding that organizational success relies at least as much on horizontal as hierarchical relationships.[140]

Citywide leaders need to have a citywide perspective and vision. They need to be able to see beyond their own roles, capacities, and organizations, and be able to cast a vision of what can be achieved through collaboration. Linden recommends five strategies for "developing a collaborative mindset in yourself and others":

1. Recruit people who are natural collaborators, take the time to interview and screen candidates well, because that will be easier than correcting their behavior afterwards;
2. Expose yourself to different cultures, fields, disciplines, and opinions, challenge your own assumptions and prejudices, and gain experience working on diverse teams;
3. Identify important outcomes that can be met only through collaborative effort and hold the team accountable;
4. Provide multiple opportunities for the team members to practice thought processes and action steps repetitively;
5. Perhaps most importantly: start with yourself, because it is not just about being a good role model, it is about demonstrating that you are serious about cross-boundary collaboration. Change starts at the top.[141]

Over the past 30 years, I have found that I must be the first person willing to learn, change, and adapt if I want to be respected and lead effectively across boundaries. It comes back to Step 1: Principles, understanding how Jesus led His diverse team on mission, and Step 2: Posture, taking on the mindset of Christ towards one another. Yet, cross-boundary partnerships can go terribly wrong, resulting in people getting hurt and relationships being broken.

Two concepts developed by Daniel Rickett I have found to be most helpful in thinking through the various levels and intricacies of partnerships are the *Alliance Continuum* and the *Model for Matching Compatibility*. The Alliance Continuum puts on an X-Y chart the level of involvement versus the level of interdependence (Figure 26). The greater the commitment of involvement, the greater the dependence of each partner on one another.

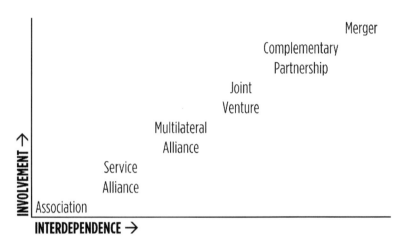

Figure 26. Alliance Continuum[142]

Rickett identifies six levels of cross-boundary partnerships that increase in involvement and interdependence as the partnership levels up. Let me describe each level with an example to illustrate each one:

Association: A step up from networks, when independent organizations affiliate with each other through agreement on a common set of values and goals. Formal membership and financial contributions may be required, for example, as with the World Evangelical Alliance.

Service Alliance: Similar to association, except that one organization is the provider of services or resources. For instance, our international church (HIF) has been blessed with a beautiful facility, which local house churches gladly make use of through a Facility Usage Contract for a small fee.

Multilateral Alliance: This partnership collaborates for a specific purpose or goal, for example as with the Love Hanoi Festival, which had many churches and organizations work together over a 15-month period.

Joint Venture: Typically, this is a short-term partnership by a few organizations to accomplish a specific project. Organizing the Long Bien cleanup project, for example, was a specific short-term joint venture project by a handful of organizations.

Complementary Partnership: In contrast with Joint Venture, this partnership has a long-term focus where each partner sees the other as "an extension of [their] own ministry." All Nations, the English service at the local Hanoi Evangelical Church, was a complementary partnership between HIF and HEC underwritten by a three-year agreement until we launched it as an independent church plant.

Merger: This unique partnership happens when two organizations are joined into one. Missio Nexus, for example, is a merger of two historic American mission associations, the IFMA and the EFMA, who merged together in 2012.[143]

Realizing the level of involvement increases simultaneously with the level of interdependence, the Alliance Continuum model helps to clarify what level of partnership you are agreeing to before getting started. The model is also helpful to identify levels of collaboration for networks, where the list of constituents may be segmented into different levels depending on the level of commitment and contribution. For example, constituents can be associated by subscribing to the newsletter, can receive benefits for a membership fee, can join efforts for a particular focus, can collaborate on a short-term project, or can join hands for long-term collaboration. Perhaps two constituents decide to merge if becoming one is more advantageous. Of course, you can choose different names for each level depending on your organizational culture and lingo. Be creative!

The higher the involvement, the more complicated the partnership becomes. This is where the second concept, Model for Matching Compatibility to Task Integration, becomes helpful in identifying to what level the partners are compatible with one another when it comes to styles of leaderships and organizational culture (see Figure 27).

Figure 27. Model for Matching Compatibility to Task Integration[144]

The partner organizations may operate with very different "operational values and ministry priorities," explains Rickett. "Operational values typically include financial practices, fundraising techniques, use of publicity, use of planning, approach to decision-making, management style, and so on."[145] Learning about each other's operational values and assessing their compatibility before committing to a higher level of partnership can avoid surprises, misunderstanding, and conflict later on in the process. Clarifying expectations on how decisions are made is particularly crucial to the success of the partner relationship. *Which decisions only need advice? Which ones can be made independently? At what level is approval or joint decision making required? Which activity requires both partners to be actively involved? When there are deadlines, how does each partner go about the decision-making process?*

Eager to partner and increase the level of collaboration, I have found myself sometimes at odds with the partner organization or individuals. In one instance, we had increased the partnership level several steps, having had success in doing smaller projects together. After a while into the long-term collaborative effort that required ongoing joint decisions and actions, I realized that our organizational practices and expectations were much more different than anticipated. When interpersonal conflict arose between team members of the complementary partnership, frustrations suddenly surfaced and ruptured, resulting in broken relationships. Although the partnership stayed intact and the project came to a successful completion, in hindsight, I wish to have had the insight of the integration vs. compatibility model and perhaps not increased the level of partnership by two or three steps, but by one. That would have given the partners a chance to familiarize themselves with each other's operational values before leveling up the partnership. This case in my context was cross-cultural, between my international team and a local team. Cross-cultural collaboration significantly increases the complexity of partnerships, which is our final topic in this chapter.

CROSS-CULTURAL PARTNERSHIPS

Unless the diversity of cross-cultural partnership is managed well, the risk of becoming less effective is much higher than single-cultural teamwork. Nancy Adler described it well:

> Culturally diverse teams often perform either more or less effectively than their single-culture counterparts. What differentiates the most effective from the least effective teams? Why are culturally diverse teams usually either more or less effective than single-culture teams but rarely equally effective? Highly-productive and less-productive teams differ in how they manage their diversity, not, as is commonly believed, in the presence or absence of diversity in the team. When well-managed, diversity becomes an asset and a productive resource for the team. When ignored, diversity causes process problems that diminish the team's productivity. Because diversity is more frequently ignored than well managed, culturally diverse teams often perform below expectations and below organizational norms.[146]

According to Adler, culturally diverse teams are more effective when the task is innovative and when the project is in its early stages.

The team leader would increase effectiveness when recognizing the differences, selects the members for their skills, generates mutual respect, values equality, focuses on the team's goal, and welcomes external feedback.[147]

This may pose quite a challenge when working cross-culturally between West-East or North-South hemispheres. Especially when the Northern/Western partner is the provider and the Southern/Eastern partner is the recipient. In those cases, the partnership will more likely tend towards a Service Alliance where there is greater dependency on the provider by the recipient. Culturally, the Southerners/Easterners may be more accommodating and prefer a telling style of leadership, whereas the Northerners/Westerners might idealize an equalitarian approach to teamwork. The Northern/Western partner will have to go out of their way to show respect, honor, and value to the Southern/Eastern partner.

I have seen this exemplified in the teamwork of the Billy Graham Evangelistic Association (BGEA). Although the organization has 60 years of experience in organizing evangelism efforts on massive scales, the staff on the ground go out of their way to show respect, honor, and value to the local church leaders. Even with American organizational culture being more top-down than European counterparts, and even though Vietnamese culture would prefer the Western experts to tell them how to do what and when, the BGEA staff went the extra mile to build up the local teams and give them decision-making power. With the highly respected reputation of Billy Graham, the BGEA staff could easily have rolled into town, told everyone what to do when and how, and organized the Love Hanoi Festival that way (but perhaps in a much less loving way!). Instead, BGEA staff repeatedly stated, "We are not here to blow in, blow up, and blow out." Unlike other mass event organizations, BGEA typically is on the ground for at least one year in advance and stays until 95% of the follow-up has been completed.

Size also matters and can result in an unbalanced partnership between a large and a small organization, especially when working cross-culturally. Large NGOs and megachurches coming from the North/West to collaborate with local churches and startups in the

East/South can skew relationships from the start. Rickett uses the illustration of an "elephant-rabbit stew." Even if the foreign partner desires an equal 50-50 partnership, "it should not surprise us that the 50-50 stew tastes more of elephant than rabbit!"[148] Half an elephant, of course, will overpower half a rabbit. The challenges can be overcome by laying down ground rules, designating alliance champions, committing to intercultural learning and understanding, building mutual trust, measuring meaningful results, documenting decisions and financials, and adjusting through feedback and reflection—which Rickett covers in-depth in *Building Strategic Relationships: A practical guide to partnering with non-western missions.*

LEADING MULTI-CULTURAL TEAMS

"Now breaks my clog!" This is a Dutch expression when you are surprised by something, as if you're so shocked that your wooden shoe even cracks! Not that the Dutch still wear wooden shoes (my brother does though), but this is how surprised I was when I discovered how Dutch I still am. I was studying a class on multinational organizations, which included books and resources on leading cross-cultural teams. Two renowned Dutch researchers, Hofstede and Trompenaars, opened my eyes to understanding the various dimensions of culture and how differing cultural values can lead to either conflict or creativity.

Leading our international church and various ministry teams made up of people from differing nationalities, I repeatedly ran into the same frustrations. My expectations and that of others differed quite a bit. When I learned about the dimensions of culture and found Hofstede's data online, I selected the data of some of my team members' cultures and was in for a shock![y] My cultural values and that of some of my teammates were almost opposite of one another—and there was not much in between. For example, Figure 28 shows two of the dimensions that greatly influence the decision-making process: Power Distance and Individualism-Collectivism.

---

[y] To download the research data by Hofstede and create your own chart, visit www. geerthofstede.com/research-and-vsm/dimension-data-matrix

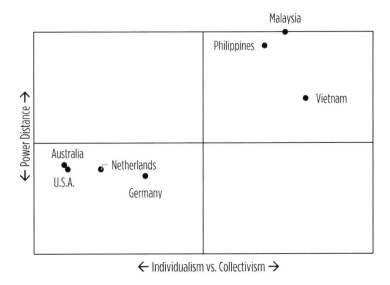

Figure 28: Comparison of two cultural dimensions for seven nationalities

Hofstede describes these two dimensions as follows:[149]

Power Distance is the extent to which the less powerful members of organizations and institutions (like the family) accept and expect that power is distributed unequally. ...Without acceptance of leadership by powerful entities, none of today's societies could run.

Individualism is the extent to which people feel independent, as opposed to being interdependent as members of larger wholes. Individualism does not mean egoism. It means that individual choices and decisions are expected. **Collectivism** does not mean closeness. It means that one "knows one's place" in life, which is determined socially.

As you can tell from the chart, I was a lot more comfortable working with teammates from cultures who had similar values, like Germans, Australians, and Americans. My Asian teammates puzzled me (this chart does *not* reflect my team at that time but illustrates my point). My Dutch culture values low power distance and high individualism. I personally do not like telling people how and when to do what but prefer a collaborative effort where everyone is part of the decision-making process. My Euro-ethnic teammates loved it, but my Asian teammates were longing for more direction, clarity, and instruction.

Adler contributed to my understanding of how different we are with her 5-step model to decision making, contrasting opposing cultural responses:[150]

1. **Problem solving:** We must change vs. we must adapt (Westerners typically identify problems long before Asians)
2. **Information search:** Gathering facts vs. going with intuition (uncertainty avoidance leads to wanting to have all the facts up front, whereas those who are comfortable with unpredictability prefer to go with the flow)
3. **Construction of alternatives:** Lifetime learning vs. adults cannot learn (some cultures believe adults stop learning at a certain age, while others value lifelong study)
4. **Choice:** Individual vs. group decision (for example, Americans value decisiveness but can change their minds, whereas Japanese value mutual agreement that stays fixed)
5. **Implementation:** quick vs. slow and top down vs. participatory (high power distance means you do not have control, so why hurry or contribute)

These two concepts, Hofstede's Cultural Dimensions and Adler's 5 Steps to Decision Making, helped me tremendously in understanding where the frustrations, tensions, misunderstandings, and conflicts were coming from. But how then do you create cultural synergy in a multicultural team? Three key practices have helped me become a more effective leader across cultures:

1. **Know yourself:** Start by learning more about your own cultural heritage, the core values that you hold on to dearly perhaps without realizing it. You may think they are Christian values and that everyone should think and behave in such a way, but likely

they are the values you were brought up with. Understanding your own biases and knowing how difficult it is to change these core cultural dimensions for yourself will give you patience and flexibility in working with others who differ from you.

2. **Know your team:** Take the time to become familiar with the culture of your team members. Share what you have learned about multicultural teamwork, show the chart displaying your team's cultural values and how they differ, and talk about them. Start with yourself by being open and transparent about the strengths and weaknesses of your cultural biases, how you can leverage them for good, and how they may hinder you in your relationships. This will set the stage for the team members to open up about their views and experiences, how they can contribute and play to one another's strengths, and perhaps even disagree with how their culture is portrayed by the researchers.

3. **Know your style:** Leadership is not fixed, there are many different styles by which people provide guidance and oversight. Knowing your preferred leaderships style and understanding the preferred leadership styles of others allows you to adjust as needed. For example, I personally prefer a selling style ("Here's the vision, you decide how"), but had to learn to be more comfortable with a telling style when needed ("Here's also the what, when, and how").

"[A]ll peoples on earth will be blessed through you," God told Abraham (Genesis 12:3). "As you go, disciple all peoples," Jesus told His followers some 2,000 years later (Matthew 28:20, paraphrase mine). Today, another 2,000 years further, this mission is still "too big to do alone and too important not to do together!"[151] God's great project of the coming kingdom and restoring all things requires partnership across all sorts of boundaries. Partnership seeks a common goal and mutual benefit, whereas networking seeks to enhance each own's benefit. Yet, networks are incubators for the seeds of partnership to sprout, grow, and bear fruit. Citywide networks connect kingdom resources with opportunities to serve and support specific segments of the city through partnership efforts. This requires collaboration across boundaries, which has the risk of being ineffective, but also the potential of being highly effective. Specifically, when leading multicultural teams, leveraging the benefits of the diversity is crucial to their success. This leads us into the next step: People. Loving your city is as effective as the leaders who facilitate the movement and the people who are gathered to seek the shalom of their city together.

CHAPTER 8

PEOPLE

Therefore if you have any encouragement from being united with Christ, if any comfort from his love, if any common sharing in the Spirit, if any tenderness and compassion, then make my joy complete by being like-minded, having the same love, being one in spirit and of one mind. Do nothing out of selfish ambition or vain conceit. Rather, in humility value others above yourselves, not looking to your own interests but each of you to the interests of the others.
Philippians 2:1-4

It was hard to believe my eyes as my wife Linda and I witnessed hundreds, even thousands, come forward in response to the gospel presentation at the Love Hanoi Festival. Who would have dreamt or imagined?! That we could experience this after 20 years of service in Hanoi was richly rewarding. It was an event, of course, but it became a moment that I and over 30,000 other people will treasure for a lifetime and into eternity. But it did not start there.

It started with a team of leaders working together in humility, valuing others above themselves, for the purpose of God's kingdom breaking through in our city. What a joy to partner with the staff of BGEA, who demonstrated "the same mindset as Christ Jesus" (Philippians 2:5). My heart was filled to overflowing, flooding my eyes then and even now, witnessing over 200 pastors holding hands in a circle during the festival's worship celebration service. Not all is perfect, but we have come a long way from a church that has survived three wars in 100 years. At the end, it is all about people. From one to three, then 12 to 72, and then from 120 to thousands.

Phill Butler was right when he stated that "*people* determine the success or failure of any collaborative effort. *By* people, *with* people, and *for* people—that's the essence of partnership."[152] At every stage, the citywide movement requires transformational leaders to facilitate the processes and partnerships for the benefit of the city and its communities. In this chapter, I will highlight the leadership skills needed for each stage of citywide movements. Going deeper, the eight perspectives of transformational leadership will be described, which the movement's leaders, staff, and volunteers need to pursue. Lastly, various models of gathering people for citywide consultations are explored. This chapter will help you identify the movement's stages, recruit the movement's leaders, and gather the movement's people.

The Movement's Stages Glenn Barth, another BGU alumnus, was inspired by Phill Butler and did his own extensive research. As a result, he developed the stages of citywide movements and described the role of the leader in his book, *The Good City: Transformed lives transforming communities.*[153] Knowing the stages and the leadership functions and skills needed to start, grow, and sustain a citywide movement gives a great advantage. We do not need to reinvent the wheel in each city, although we cannot blindly copy and paste either. Learning the principles and processes and learning from the mistakes and successes of other citywide movements is invaluable.

The six stages of citywide movements are Exploration, Formation, Operation, Realization, Transformation, and Replication. Each stage has its specific function with a goal to move to the next stage. The leadership skills required at each stage changes as the movement grows and matures (see Table 3). It is possible that one leader can learn, adapt, and change along with the movement's progress. It may also be that different leaders are needed at different stages. A leader certainly would not want the movement to stagnate due to their resistance to either change or pass on the baton. This section will give a brief overview of each stage and is adapted from Barth's chapter on Understanding Transformation Stages.

Table 3: Stages of Development for Organizations Serving City Movements[154]

STAGE	FUNCTION	SKILL
1. Exploration	Catalyst Visionary	Relational Communication Convening
2. Formation	Visionary	Communication Facilitating Management Creative Thinking
3. Operation	Management	Decision Making People Building Motivational
4. Realization	Prayer	Doing the right things at the right time
5. Transformation	Discipling	Presence-based prayer
6. Replication	Teaching	Training Coaching

   1. EXPLORATION: To start a Love [Your City] movement, a leader with a heart and vision for collaboration is needed who can be the catalyst of the cross-sector partnership. The catalyst tirelessly meets with individuals and groups to learn, connect, and share the vision. Yet, one person cannot go far, so soon enough the catalyst needs to form a catalytic team. This may result from organizing a catalytic event or growing the team one person at a time. The catalytic team, also called *Envisioning Team*[155] or *Servant Leadership Team,*[156] is focused on the task of exploring. This will include gathering initial information and doing initial interviews, reviewing the information before continuing interviews, after which initial conclusions are made.[157] Leveraging existing ministry networks (marketplace, students, leadership, non-profit, teachers, etc.) can jumpstart the exploration stage. The leader at this stage needs to excel in relational and communication skills, as well as being able to convene meetings and gatherings.

In Hanoi, the Love Hanoi Festival was the catalytic event that brought all the churches together and gave birth to the Love in Action team. When the event was over, however, the structure and motivation dwindled. Right now, we are restarting the Love in Action team, forming focus groups to explore each of the seven domains of society. There are a few groups already in existence such as Alpha Youth, WOL Marketplace Ministry, Christian Medical Fellowship, as well as some dormant networks that need to be reengaged. The goal at the end of the Exploratory stage for the Love in Action team is to publish the findings in a booklet that can be distributed to church leaders and members citywide so that everyone can have the same information.

2. FORMATION: The formation stage is focused on creating a coalition strong enough to move on to the Operation stage. The leader's focus will be on vision casting, utilizing skills such as communication, facilitating, management, and creative thinking. Key influential leaders need to be gathering in order to create the buy-in for their ongoing support. Objectives and expectations need to be clarified up front. The leader and the team need to carefully plan and facilitate this gathering. Time and space need to be created for information sharing and relationship building. Once everyone is on the same page, a decision to move forward to the Operation stage can be made. The support of the influencers is critical as funding and staffing will come from their churches and organizations. The goals and strategy need to be endorsed at this higher level of leadership for the team to be empowered and enabled for operation.

3. OPERATION: What used to be an informal, decentralized, relational network, now enters a stage of formalization and organization. Not every citywide movement makes it to this stage, which may be for the best. Love Boulder in Colorado continued to be a relational network, an idea, a phrase often repeated to inspire and motivate, but never an organization. Unite! in Atlanta, Georgia, formalized the network but did not centralize or staff the operations. Love Singapore organized annual prayer summits but did not spread out into other domains. Each city's context is unique, so every movement needs to take shape as determined in the Formation stage.

Whichever form the operation takes on, it is important to continue exploring as well as staying fairly decentralized. The leader's skills focus on decision making, people building, and motivation. Managing the diversity of decentralized teams is critical for ongoing effectiveness As Barth points out, "Those who have sought to build a centralized organization where a person or council keeps track of and directs activities for Christians in a city or community have limited the effectiveness of the effort by reducing both the number of participants and the diversity of interests that could be engaged."[158]

One helpful concept at this stage is that of centered set vs. bounded set thinking. Denominations and most churches are typified by bounded set thinking. People who agree with their statements of faith, dogmas, cultures, and practices are insiders, others are outsiders. This is illustrated by a closed circle. To have leaders and members of various churches and denominations working together, the thinking must shift to a centered set, where the focus is on the mission or cause (see Figure 29).

The team needs a minimal set of beliefs and values that the partners and staff agree to (such as the Lausanne Covenant[z]). However, the team can collaborate with anyone who cares about the same causes and share common values. Within the movement, networks and groups can form around the various causes pursued by the team. This is how a movement maintains decentralization (see Figure 30). This way, Christians and churches can be a witness not only to those they are serving, but also to the partner organizations they are working with. Working alongside non-Christians for the common good open up many opportunities for spiritual conversations, as illustrated earlier in the chapter on Process.

---

[z] To learn more about the Lausanne covenant, visit https://www.lausanne.org/content/covenant/lausanne-covenant

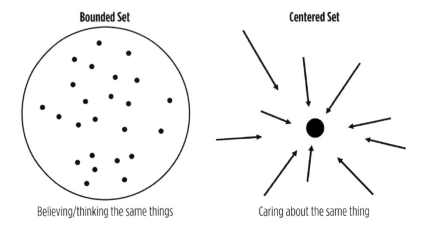

Figure 29: Bounded set vs. centered set thinking[159]

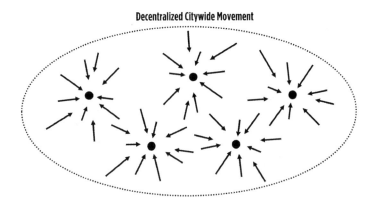

Figure 30: Decentralized citywide movement organized around causes[160]

4. REALIZATION: At this stage, things can get exciting! When God starts to work through the citywide movement and demonstrates His favor by blessing the projects and the people, it is time to celebrate. It is important to keep in mind what is considered a breakthrough or success. Pastors tend to count churches and converts, to see God's "name glorified" (Matthew 6:9). But from a kingdom perspective, all progress towards seeing God's "kingdom come and will be done" is success (Matthew 6:10).

Reduced crime rate, fewer school dropouts, families staying together, racial reconciliation, cleaner environments, increased care for the elderly, and other external metrics outside of church life should be celebrated. When God's kingdom becomes reality and people see it demonstrated, the heavenly Father will receive the glory (Matthew 5:16).

Prayer is key to seeing the kingdom of God breaking through into our world. The focus during this stage is to organize and mobilize prayer summits, prayer walks, prayer gatherings, congregational prayer, and personal prayer. Pray on site, pray at work, pray in church, pray at home, and pray while driving. Prayer should be an ongoing effort integrated from the start, but it is critical to bring kingdom realization. It is through the power of prayer that the movement can transition to the next stage: Transformation.

5. TRANSFORMATION: When God's kingdom breaks through, families, communities, cities, and societies can be completely transformed. Shalom will be evident in homes, on the streets, at schools, in the workplace, in hospitals, in government offices, and every in nook and cranny. The great revival movements of the past were the instigators of internationally renowned universities and hospitals, and of anti-slavery and women's rights movements. Bars were closed and theaters turned into churches. Morality increased and God's presence was experienced in almost every home.[161] The film *The Transformations: A Documentary* by George Otis Jr.[162] illustrates such complete community transformations in different continents of the world.

Discipleship and presence-based prayer are the focus of this stage. New believers need to be matched with mature Christians to be discipled in their faith and mentored in their newfound life. Without discipleship, the fruit of transformation will be lost, choked, overwhelmed, not unrooted, and not bear fruit.

6. REPLICATION: When Christians in other cities hear about the kingdom realization and community transformation experienced, they will come to see it for themselves and would want to take it back to their own cities. For example, in the year 2000, church leaders in Little Rock, Arkansas, organized a week-long Sharefest event which drew over 100 churches and resulted in 3,000+ volunteers serving in 105 service projects. Within a ten-year period, Sharefest had been replicated in 50 cities throughout the USA and globally.[163]

Replication is very motivating but can also become distracting if the movement leader and team are not careful to stay the course. Early success can draw the leader and staff away from building the momentum of their movement by training others to start their movements. The temptation can also be to copy the programs of one movement to another city and expect the same results. This was the case with the launch of Love HCMC (Ho Chi Minh City). An enthusiastic team from HCMC had heard of Love Hanoi and seen the early successes. Quickly they had copied the logo, website, T-shirts, notebooks, and banners to launch Love HCMC at an event, of which I was the main speaker. Afterwards, however, the early excitement was lost. Starting and leading a movement proved to take a lot more work and a dedicated catalytic leader.

Not all was lost, however, as the event did impact believers, churches, and organizations. One organization decided to read *A Theology as Big as the City* for staff devotions and the following year changed their strategic focus from provincial to urban. It completely transformed the staff and the organizational culture, now that they were loving their neighbors instead of distant "recipients." Today, the team that launched Love HCMC also launched Love in Action for the Love Spring Festival, organized in collaboration with BGEA, to be held in 2021. Working together with the team in Hanoi, Love in Action will become a national network with Love [Your City] movements in many cities throughout Vietnam, Lord willing!

THE MOVEMENT'S LEADERS

Founded by Ray Bakke and his family, the Bakke Graduate University (BGU) upholds eight perspectives of transformational leadership which are biblical, practical, and countercultural.[164] These you will not find in popular leadership books on the shelves in bookstores, although some principles may be comparable. They also may not lead to success as defined by worldly standards. They are reflective of and modeled by Christ, whose urban ministry ended with incarceration, torture, and death. This does not make a bestselling leadership book although the Bible has always been an all-time bestseller! The price of reconciliation was paid for upon the cross, which then led to the ultimate transformation: resurrection. To see true transformation take place in our cities and communities, the leaders, staff, and volunteers of the movement would do well to clothe themselves with these eight perspectives of Christlike leadership.

1. CALLING-BASED LEADERSHIP: The leader pursues a life of calling to be used by God in His transformational kingdom work in the city. The work will be challenging and the disappointments inevitable, there will be setbacks and disagreements to work through, it will take years for the movement to take shape and become self-sustaining. All these will be offset by the excitement of seeing the fruit of the leader's labor. Yet a strong sense of calling is needed to overcome the obstacles and not to get carried away by successes.

2. INCARNATIONAL LEADERSHIP: Having "the same mindset as Christ" (Philippians 2:5), the leader seeks to identify with the plights, hopes, and experiences of those he is reaching to help. The leader does not just go *to* and do things *for* the community, but lives *in* the city and the neighborhood, working *with* civic leaders as well as the residents. The agenda of the leader must be clear: He is there to serve. It can be tempting, however, to idealize incarnational ministry to such an extreme that it becomes an impossible standard to uphold. This idealization can create great tension in the leader's thinking, within the team, and in their families.

Viv Grigg, founder of Servant Partners, an organization that places missionaries to serve incarnationally within slums around the world, observed that a prolonged time of such extreme adaptation can have negative effects on the missionary and the family members. "The Protestant missions to whom I have sent workers have burned them out within a year," Grigg wrote to me in a personal email. "Catholic order set up committed caring communities. Protestants set up works. Workers in slums burn out. ... Incarnational living is not an ideal. It is a limited reality, towards an ideal. Along the way we remain bicultural and damaged and need rest." Therefore, Viv recommends, "Retreating is the best form of advance. ... In the rhythm of work and rest and communal worship, where the Holy Spirit is the capacity for sustained engagement." Those who are bitter and traumatized should not be sent. "Poets do better than achievers," Viv wrote. "A 4.0 GPA is a dangerous thing. Perfectionism got such people through school, but perfectionism does not make for a capacity to accommodate to difficult chaotic environments." So, who should go? "The balanced make the best church planters, not the most gifted, because it is a multiplex leadership dynamic."[165]

For 13 years my family lived in normal alleyways of Hanoi neighborhoods, until I could not cope any longer with the noise pollution, the lack of sunlight, the exposure to burglary, and the confined living spaces. We were ready to leave when the Lord made it clear we were to stay. My decision was firm; we needed to move to an international development with open space designs, gardens, security, and limited construction hours. "If You want us to stay, You have to pay," was my deal with God. It made all the difference and now we're ten years further down the road. This created another tension, however, because I felt like we were not living incarnationally enough—even though we were still in Hanoi. Lowell Bakke's teaching and Viv Grigg's writing about the role of the international church and the affluent helped me a great deal to overcome the dichotomous thinking of idealizing incarnational ministry to the detriment of the missionary (more in the next chapter).

3. REFLECTIVE LEADERSHIP: Perhaps you have met leaders who lack self-awareness and seemingly are not in touch with reality. Reflective leaders not only are committed to lifelong learning, but also to introspection and contemplation. They invite critical feedback from others about themselves, their methods and models, and their communication and style. Leading by example, leaders become catalysts more by what they do than what they say. Launching a citywide movement is not go-go-go but learn-go-learn-go-learn-go. Reflection needs to be integrated at every level: leadership, teams, consultations, communications, projects, and services. Implement a quality control survey as often as possible to maintain a posture of learning, staying relevant and nimble as a leader and an organization.

4. SERVANT LEADERSHIP: Although this concept was popularized by Robert Greenleaf's book, *Servant Leadership,* it was Christ who set the ultimate example. Teaching His disciples on leadership, Jesus stated that He had "not come to be served, but to serve, and to give his life as a ransom for many" (Matthew 20:28). Wrapping a towel around His waist and washing His disciples' feet, Jesus explained, "I have set you an example that you should do as I have done for you" (John 13:15). Like Jesus, the leader "leads by serving and serves by leading."[166] Government and citizens alike may watch the leader to see if the "hidden agenda" will come to the surface over time. Trust will be gained if the leader demonstrates the altruistic posture of Christ, valuing others above self and looking out for the interest of others (Philippians 2:4).

5. CONTEXTUAL LEADERSHIP: "Contextualization means doing theology ourselves," said Dr. Tim Gener, President of the Asian Theological Seminary. Christians have "the right to articulate the evangelical traditions in their own terms in light of their own issues."[167] The outcome of a reflective, incarnational leader is the contextualization of theology and theories in the local community. Models should not be copied and pasted from other cities, countries, and continents, but adapted to and developed in the local context. Contextual leaders recognize that God has long been at work in the community and the city long before they caught on to the idea of urban transformation. Like Father Beltran, the leader seeks to discover where Jesus already is and how the gospel is uniquely expressed in that context (see Step 2: Posture).

6. GLOBAL LEADERSHIP: Not only is the leader tuned into the local context, but also into the global complexity of the Church, economics, politics, thought, and trends. The leader must have a centered set of thinking, not locked into their own church paradigm or denominational dogmas. The leader must be reading and learning widely, participating in global networks and gatherings, conversing with peers and with people unlike them, and connecting their local movement with global associations.

Personally, I have been largely enriched by the comradery of peers across denominational, geographical, and cultural boundaries in the Urban Shalom Society (USS).[aa] The society in turn engages with the

---

[aa] For more information visit www.urbanshalomsociety.org

United Nations Human Settlements Programme (UN Habitat) and has built a platform to speak into the New Urban Agenda.[ab] The official UN Habitat Multi-Faith Urban Thinkers Campus (UTC) is holding forums on every continent organized by USS.

In 2018, I joined the society at UN Habitat's World Urban Forum in Kuala Lumpur, Malaysia. Over 25,000 people had come from across the globe to discuss the future of the city. In the next 30 years, the urban infrastructure will double and house 75% of the world's population. Can you imagine that? Yet, there we were, the only Christian group of about 25 practitioners trying to enter a global conversation that purposefully avoids talking about religion and faith. Where were all the Christians? Where is the Church in this crucial conversation?

7. SHALOM LEADERSHIP: Urban transformation happens when restoration and reconciliation occur. Using the transformed relationships model of shalom introduced in Step 1: Principles, the leader seeks to reconcile people with God, self, others, the community, and the environment. "The leader works towards the well-being, abundance, and wholeness of the community, as well as individuals."[168] This is why we can join UN Habitat under their motto, "Cities 2030, cities for all." Building trust and mutual understanding among church leaders, between church and city leaders, and between Christians and their communities is a great step towards reconciling and normalizing relationships. Working together on common good projects fosters and reinforces such relationships. The leader, then, must be a person of peace and a peacemaker, even though they, like everyone else, are on a journey towards complete reconciliation and restoration. As Eric Swanson told me personally, we must add "whole person" to the "whole church, whole gospel, and whole city" slogan. The leader must be willing to undergo the process of repentance and forgiveness before challenging others to do likewise.

One example of a shalom leader is Joseph Nyamutera, who experienced the atrocities of the Rwandan genocide. Joseph now has a message for people who want to experience God's reconciliation for them personally, with others, and with the world. From childhood, Joseph felt worthless,

---

[ab] Download the New Urban Agenda at www.unhabitat.org

lost in the middle of 11 siblings, the sixth child of a rigid, abusive father and an overwhelmed mother whose complaints about the children brought swift and violent retribution from their father. As the struggles between the Hutu and Tutsi tribes of Rwanda escalated, Joseph adopted the ethnic views of his peers. As a Hutu, it was easy to blame all of society's problems on the Tutsi. They became the enemy. As a pastor, Joseph preached against the hatred and violence. He even helped wounded Tutsi escape Rwanda to safety, at great danger to himself and his family. Yet secretly, he celebrated Hutu victories and the anonymous Tutsi deaths. For two years, Joseph's family stayed in Goma's refugee camp of one million people.

The turning point from hopelessness came unexpectedly when he volunteered with his church to clean rooms at a seminar on "trauma healing." Attendance was low, so Joseph was asked to listen to the presentation, mainly to encourage the British speaker and her Tutsi translator. That day, Joseph Nyamutera found reconciliation for himself with God. "I discovered God as Father. I received much healing from my harsh upbringing and could forgive my own father." It was only the beginning. Later, Joseph was invited for further training in reconciliation ministry. For the next 18 years, Joseph and his Tutsi brother-in-Christ Anastase have presented more than 300 seminars. "All over the country, we have brought together pastors, students, women, orphans, social workers, soldiers, youth, children ... We have ministered inside and outside of Rwanda, among Rwandan exiles, Congolese, Burundians, South Africans, Europeans ..."[169] If those involved in the Rwanda genocide can repent, forgive, and become shalom leaders, so can anyone.

8. PROPHETIC LEADERSHIP: When it comes to broken systems and practices at the macro level of society, prophetic leadership is needed to speak to those in power and to speak with power. This power comes from the sense of calling, incarnational posture, reflective practice, servant attitude, contextualized theology, global connections, and a shalom framework. The truth must be spoken in love (Ephesians 4:15), both inside and outside the church. Specifically, the prophetic leader must "[s]peak up for those who cannot speak for themselves, for the rights of all who are destitute. Speak up and judge fairly; defend the rights of the poor and needy" (Proverbs 31:8-9). The leader must defend the plight of the least, the last, and the lost.

Management skills, leadership styles, and teamwork can be studied in numerous schools and resources, but the eight perspectives of transformational leadership just outlined are a rare combination of biblical principles often overlooked or even despised. The movement's leadership team must exhibit, grow, and steward these characteristics through honest self-reflection and feedback. In the process and at the end, it is not about the leader, but about the people. The "know-it-all" and "do-it-all" type of leader will not succeed. It is not about information and motivation, but about transformation, as Ray Bakke learned the hard way.

THE MOVEMENT'S PEOPLE

Over a period of ten years during the 1980s, Ray Bakke visited and consulted 200 cities, working in partnership with the Lausanne Committee for World Evangelization and with World Vision. In the beginning, Ray thought, *"If they just had the correct information and motivation, they could turn their city around."*[170] After about 50 cities, Ray came to a shocking realization that the major barriers to city transformation lay not with the city itself, but with the church! During one session in Cairo, Ray came to understand that

> the pastors were intimidated by their own church congregations, which might think them silly and send them packing; or by their boards, which might think them crazy and cut off funds for favorite projects; or by their denominational leaders, who might frown on doing something radical and blacklist these pastors from climbing the denominational ladder. I heard these fine ministers say things such as, "Our bishops would never let us do that," "Nobody would fund that," "Seminary did not prepare me for this."[171]

As a result, Bakke focused on designing process-driven consultations that were "rooted in relationships across the city." Consultations "connect the powerful with the powerless, and people of need with people of resource ... people who have learned by experience with professors who are instilling the next generation of emerging leaders."[172] Consultations turn cities into learning labs.

In this section, seven types of consultations as developed by Bakke and Sharpe (see Table 4) are described to provide a variety of methods to gather people for citywide movements.

Table 4: Methods of gathering people for citywide movements[173]

Love [Your City] Conference:	celebrate signs of hope, address most pressing issues
Love [Your City] Tour:	expose church members, leaders, pastors to the city
New Leaders Orientation:	introduce to civic leaders, ministries, congregations
Urban Think Tank:	one issue, sharing, present papers, action steps
Academic Seminars:	one week, lectures and immersion, academic credit
Denominational Consultation:	assess urban ministry nationally and internationally
Three-Day Consultation:	citywide catalyst for creating partnerships & initiatives

LOVE [YOUR CITY] CONFERENCE: This is a full day or half day gathering of ministry leaders from across the city to celebrate the signs of hope of what God is doing in the various sectors. The purpose is to gather church, ministry, and city leaders, to listen to one another, to inspire participants to join and start new initiatives, and to network the leaders for potential partnerships. The conference could be a large all-day event once a year or organized quarterly or even more frequently around very specific topics.

The conference can be themed around a domain or a specific issue that is pertinent for the city at that time, such as environment, at risk children, poverty, social entrepreneurship, drug addiction, homelessness, education, governance, health care, etc. Considering the domains of society, the organizing team can spend time researching one domain prior to the summit, discover the needs and opportunities, network the various players, and invite inspiring role models to share their vision and best practices. The conference presents a huge opportunity to specifically invite city government or domain leaders to speak into the life of the citywide church. Using TED talks as an example, the presentations need to be short, engaging, and inspiring, so that a variety of presenters can share in a short amount of time.[174] Forming discussion groups afterwards around topics of interest or even around each presenter will ensure the participants are engaged and come away with action steps and network connections.

Referred to earlier, in Hanoi we have called these events *Love Hanoi Conferences,* which we organize twice a year on Saturday afternoons. Appendix A outlines the roles and schedule for one of these conferences as an example. Appendix B gives the guidelines for presenters, and Appendix C lists the survey questions we use to evaluate our conference. We sell a variety of Love Hanoi promotional products (polos, T-shirts, notebooks, mugs, hats, pens, wristbands, etc.) during the conference and give a free pen or sticker in return for handing in the survey. Branding is an important part of inspiring people with the vision and idea, making it stick, and promoting the campaign.

LOVE [YOUR CITY] TOUR: We had great fun hopping on the bus and visiting various partner organizations during our CityPartners Tour in Hanoi. Starting off in a social enterprise café, the group bussed over to visit a restaurant operated by the deaf and blind, then made a stop at the historical local church to learn from the pastor there, and ended up having lunch on the Red River with another agency leader sharing their heart. In Boulder, Colorado, the pastors organized what they called "The Magic Bus Tour" to get the Love Boulder campaign started.[175] In one day, they visited eight agencies that provided community services, learning first-hand how the church could partner with them to help the homeless, runaway youth, HIV/AIDS victims, etc. In Fresno, California, pastors were invited by the Police Chief to ride along with the police officers to experience the challenges they faced each day and night. This totally transformed the perspectives of the pastors who joined the "Cops and Clergy Ride Along" and led them to actively love their city![176]

This is a great way to expose new (and long-time) church members, ministry leaders, and local pastors to the city. The tour can start off with an introduction to a theology for the city, the city's history and demographics, and an overview of what God is doing through His kingdom work. Then, hopping on a bus, the group can visit various partner organizations, key churches, important sites, to get an in-person experience and gain a love for their city. If there is a social enterprise running a café or restaurant, then have coffee and lunch there! Along the way, perhaps in the bus or while walking around, the group can pray for the needs and opportunities they encounter. At the end, the debriefing will allow individuals to share their impressions and follow-up with action steps. Sharpe offers some helpful questions for reflection during the day: "What does God see in this city? What breaks God's heart? What gives God joy? What can God use here and what would God like to clean up?"[177]

NEW LEADER'S ORIENTATION: New pastors and ministry leaders can be quickly integrated into the existing network with a city orientation program designed for them. New churches are planted, existing churches change pastors, ministries and organizations change leaders—there is always an influx of new leaders in the city. On their own, it might take years to build the relationships and gain the insights received during this orientation. Like the city tour, the orientation may include visiting civic leaders, significant ministries, exemplary churches, underserved neighborhoods.

URBAN THINK TANK: Focused around one urban issue, the Urban Think Tank gathers specialists, academics, and ministry leaders with expertise in the area of focus. More formal in approach, presenters are requested to write papers in advance for their presentation and for publication. Participants will be asked to prepare by reading books and/ or articles prior to meeting.

On the day of meeting itself, after the presentations have been made, discussion groups work towards creating a report to be made and distributed to the larger group. At the end, the facilitator works with the group to formulate action steps agreed upon by all. This may be formulated as a declaration, which often come out of think tank meetings and frequently include the name of the location where they met and/or the issue discussed, such as the *Declaration of Santiago on the Sustainable Development Goals,*[178] or the well-known *Lausanne Covenant.* The papers and reports are combined and published in digital or paper booklet format for wider distribution.

ACADEMIC SEMINARS: A standard practice of Bakke Graduate University (BGU), academic seminars are one-week events for students and practitioners who desire to gain academic credit or to gain further exposure. Filled with lectures by professors, presentations by practitioners, site visits to ministries, group discussions with peers, and immersion experiences in underserved communities, the seminar is truly an enriching and life-changing experience. Such academic seminars are hosted in cities like Hong Kong, Manila, Kuala Lumpur, Singapore, Beirut, Amman, Jerusalem, Fresno, Pittsburgh, New York City, and hopefully in Hanoi soon!

Having participated in the Manila academic seminar, it was a transformational experience for me coming out of Hanoi. Although still in Asia, Manila is a totally different city in a nation that is known as the most Christian in the continent. Yet, the urban issues are extreme due to the corruption of every layer and sector of society. With 95% of the country's population considering themselves Christian, how can 50% of the city live in urban slums? Brave Christian leaders, among them some very short but very courageous women, have pioneered urban ministries that have grown into nationwide institutions, including banks! I highly recommend participating in a week-long academic seminar with BGU[ac] or with the Ray Bakke Centre for Urban Transformation in Hong Kong.[ad]

DENOMINATIONAL CONSULTATION: In addition to citywide consultations, which gathers churches from multiple denominational affiliations together with non-denominational churches, consultations can also be held for a whole denomination to help refocus their urban vision and strategy. Each denomination has its own strengths, histories, and unique contributions to the kingdom of God. The consultants come alongside denominational leaders to assess their urban ministries nationally and internationally. Time would be spent listening to the urban experiences of the city pastors within the denomination. Models

---

[ac] Visit https://www.bgu.edu/students/course-list/educational-experiences/

[ad] Visit http://rbc.bethelhk.org/index.php?lang=en

of urban ministry can be introduced, including "the values of the whole church, whole gospel, and whole city ... encouraging them to partner with, rather than compete with each other."[179] Older denominations can be rejuvenated by connecting with their roots while developing emerging urban ministries.

THREE-DAY CONSULTATION: Gathering a larger group (100-200) of key people in the city, the three-day consultation aims to surface the real pressing issues of the city, design programs to address those issues, and identify the major barriers for implementation. At the end, everyone has a greater perspective of the needs, ministries, and opportunities to have the whole church bring the whole gospel to the whole city. The three-day consultation then becomes a citywide catalyst for creating partnerships and launch new initiatives. A sample program is listed in Appendix D.

The Love [Your City] movement is all about people, from the leaders to the staff to the volunteers to the city's authorities and citizens alike. From the start, the movement requires a catalytic leader and team to ignite the engine and get it running. As the movement gains momentum, different leadership skills are needed at each stage of the journey. The leaders should celebrate early successes, but not let these become a distraction once other cities' leaders show interest in receiving training. Staying the course, with prayer and power in the Holy Spirit, the movement will see God's kingdom to realization in the city as it is in heaven. It takes a unique perspective of transformational leadership to reach this point and move towards transformation and replication. Having the same mindset of Jesus Christ, leaders exhibit the eight qualities described in this chapter. Utilizing various models of consultations, the movement will grow from 12 to 120 to thousands and (prayerfully) millions.

The five steps of citywide movements hopefully have inspired you to get started or to keep going. Perhaps you are in the starting blocks ready to run, but where and how do you begin? That is what Chapter 9, Love [Your City] Too! is all about. So go to the next page and let's get started!

PART THREE:

IT'S YOUR TURN!

CHAPTER 9

LOVE [YOUR CITY] TOO!

*Does anyone dare despise this day of small
beginnings? They'll change their tune when they
see Zerubbabel setting the last stone in place!*

Zechariah 4:10 (MSG)

I still remember my first conversation with Dr. Brad Smith, President
of Bakke Graduate University, when we spoke over the phone as I was
contemplating embarking on the doctoral program to support the
launch and development of our Love Hanoi campaign. To me it sounded
impossible, ridiculous, unbelievable when he challenged me to consider
writing my dissertation with the city government as my audience; that
my final project would result in a citywide gathering of leaders from every
domain, including government leaders, during which I would present my
paper to them. "Yeah right," I told him, as I could not believe such an
outcome would be possible. My reply to Dr. Smith was that I would just
begin and be faithful in the process, wherever this may lead to. The rest is
history, and you have read some of that history in this book.

As HIF was inspired by the Love Boulder story, today other
international and national churches around the world have launched or
are about to launch their Love [Your City] campaigns: Love HCMC, Love
Danang, Love Bac Giang, Love Phuket, Love Bangkok, Love Dubai, Love
Havertown, Love … ? We probably don't even know who is thinking about
it or has already started. Perhaps, after reading this book, you also would
like to launch your own Love [Your City] campaign. Whether you are a
pastor, Christian leader, student, missionary, or whatever your role may

be in God's kingdom, together with others, by the empowerment of the Holy Spirit, you can begin today!

This concluding chapter will highlight some ideas for you to get started in launching your own Love [Your City] initiative. After a brief word of encouragement, I will reflect on some lessons learned throughout the process, describe the role of international and affluent churches in citywide movements, and summarize the principles described in this book. At the end, I will give a few recommendations for how to begin or how to continue if you have already started a similar initiative. The five steps may seem like giant leaps, but it is OK to first dip your toes in to test the waters.

DO NOT DESPISE SMALL BEGINNINGS

After my call with BGU's president, I was reminded by a sermon I had heard by Pastor Joshua Finley at Elim Gospel Church based on Zechariah 4:10, "Do not despise small beginnings." When the first group of Israelites returned from their exile in Babylon to their home country, Jerusalem was still a disaster zone. Not unlike Ground Zero in New York City, the temple had been completely burned down and destroyed just to pry out every sliver of gold from the walls, doors, and furnishings. The first building project of the returnees was to restore the temple from the foundation up. This had been commanded and funded by King Cyrus, the new emperor of the Persian empire which had defeated and succeeded the Assyrians. Under capable leadership of Joshua the priest and Zerubbabel the governor, the temple's rebuilding project had begun soon after their return to Jerusalem in 538 BC.

Despite the favor of King Cyrus and God's sovereign provisions provided through the king, it did not take long before the people were discouraged. Those who had been born in Babylon were excited, but those who had seen the previous temple built by Solomon wept for the foundation's smaller footprint. It was through Zechariah, a priest turned prophet, that God spoke words of admonishment and encouragement to his people and to Zerubbabel specifically. "This is the word of the Lord to Zerubbabel: 'Not by might nor by power, but by my Spirit,' says the Lord Almighty" (Zechariah 4:6). Often quoted as encouragement to one another, this prophetic word helped Zerubbabel not to compare himself with other leaders and his predecessors (King David and King Solomon), but that the work was purely the Holy Spirit's doing. The obstacles, which may seem like unsurmountable mountains, will become like level ground before Zerubbabel. He had laid the foundations, he will complete the project, and will "bring out the capstone to shouts of "God bless it! God bless it!" (v. 7-9). Then, to boost Zerubbabel's spirit and the people's motivation, the Lord said, "For whoever has despised the day of small [beginnings] shall rejoice and shall see the plumb line in the hand of Zerubbabel" (v. 10, ESV).

HINDSIGHT IS 20/20: LESSONS LEARNED

Two years into the Love Hanoi campaign, I read Butler's book *Well Connected* and I highlighted 12 principles in my study paper, *From Exploration to Formation*. At that point, I was anticipating what we should be doing next. Things turned out quite different than expected—and for the better—as we relied on God's guidance for this kingdom project. I will now use these same principles to look back and reflect on what I have learned in the process. "Hindsight is 20/20," as the saying goes, so 2020 is a good year to look back!

TO START, ONLY FEW ARE NEEDED: "Don't wait to start until you have 'everybody' you want or need!" Butler wrote.[180] You do not need every pastor and ministry leader in the room to get started. Before calling a meeting with key leaders, you can start with just a handful of people (preferably of different genders, churches, denominations, and organizations) to form a team, start testing and practicing the ideas, and prepare for the vision casting meeting with key leaders. You only "need *a few* of the [key] leaders or ministries already recognized as credible and competent in the field," even 30-50% is enough.[181] The reason is that you want "people with a vision for the outcomes, committed to the idea of God's people working together."[182] If you invite leaders who might be resistant, late adopters, or overpowering, it can jeopardize the partnership at the start. You may want to wait with inviting lead pastors of large churches and organizations as they may have too much influence or may be used to have things run their way (remember the "elephant-rabbit stew" story from Step 4: Partner?). However, like in the case of Perimeter Church and Unity! network, a large church with a humble posture can become the catalyst of the movement!

In Hanoi, the Love Hanoi campaign was initiated by HIF, which in comparison to house churches is large, foreign, and affluent. By demonstrating ongoing service to and with local churches, and through the Love Hanoi Festival, we were able to shift the ownership of Love Hanoi to churches citywide. I worked with a few key leaders in the early years until I was invited by all the top leaders to chair the Love in Action committee for the festival. After the festival, I presented the vision for Love in Action's ongoing ministry citywide and nationwide to these same leaders. They not only provided great feedback, but also gave their endorsement, which in Vietnamese culture is key to recruiting their church members for volunteers and staff.

RELATIONSHIPS OF TRUST ARE KEY: "All durable, effective partnerships are built on trust and whole relationships."[183] Biblical partnerships come to mind, such as David and Jonathan, Joshua and Caleb, Ruth and Naomi, Esther and Mordecai, Ezra and Nehemiah, Barnabas and Paul, Paul and Priscilla and Aquila, and so on. Sadly, in the kingdom of God there is not always a high culture of trust between leaders. History may give good reasons for mistrust and the country's context may be a low-trust culture. Trust is key, however, to launch a collaborative effort. Start out with trusted coworkers in Christ and then invest the time to build trust among leaders citywide. It will take a lot of coffee and food to build relationships of trust, often one-on-one or with a few together at first (but who wouldn't mind more coffee and food?!). Trust can be built by serving one another and serving others together.

Vietnam's history of wars and mistrust has made the country a difficult context for building trust among leaders in every sector of society, even between family members and in marriages. This low-trust culture has also been prevalent among church leaders. Sometimes overseas mission agencies and denominations have made it worse by having local pastors choose sides, creating dependency on foreign resources (obviously not familiar with Asset Based Community Development), and "buying" church plants so they could include the numbers in their mission reports.

As an international church, HIF has demonstrated that unity across denominational, social, professional, national, and cultural diversity is not only possible but even produces a dynamic church experience. HIF supports ministry projects of churches from any denomination and welcomes any church group to utilize our facilities. This posture of generosity and collaboration has fostered trust to the point that HIF has become a neutral space for citywide church leaders to gather, pray, and discuss joint projects.

THE VISION MUST BE GREATER: "Partnerships are durable, effective, and usually strategic when they are driven by a great vision."[184] To echo Missio Nexus once more, "The Great Commission is too big for anyone to accomplish alone and too important not to try to do together."[185] The vision must be a "God idea" and "God-sized" in "God's timing" to inspire participation and collaboration. The vision must outlast the leaders' lifetime and their term of service in leadership. If the vision can be fulfilled by yourself and/or your church or organization and within your lifetime, it is too small. Sadly, many ministry leaders have been trained to think small, to think not much bigger than the 200 or so people they will pastor, to be confined by a poverty mentality of fundraising. We have made the gospel small, pertaining to individual salvation, and the world's problems seemingly too big. "We need to think big about the gospel [and] small about the world's problems." says Missio Nexus.[186] Through missional partnerships we can tackle the world's greatest problems with the best news ever.

It was not until the Asia director of BGEA called upon Hanoi's pastors to host a citywide festival that all Christian leaders were willing to work together. The vision was greater than we could have thought of or imagined—a God idea. It was also bigger than anyone could have accomplished alone—God-sized. The timing was right as well, following up on previous events and building on the city government's favor—God's timing! Yet, I have said that it was still too small and too short-term. "The festival is over, but Jesus still loves Hanoi!" was my challenge to the leaders at the closing ceremony. Sometimes it requires an outside leader and an outside organization, like BGEA, to cast a large enough vision and draw all the leaders together. At the end, however, the vision must be owned by the leaders themselves, otherwise the vision will leave along with the outsider. A lesson Nehemiah had to learn also.

PRAYER IS ESSENTIAL: "Our partnerships must be informed and empowered by God's Holy Spirit in order to be effective."[187] As God spoke to Zerubbabel, so He speaks to us: Citywide movements cannot be accomplished by our might or power, but only by His Spirit. Prayer is like the life-giving blood that flows through our bodies and the Spirit is like our heart that pumps it through. Without either, we would be dead! Prayer events, prayer gathering, prayer times, prayer guidelines, prayer bookmarks, prayer devotionals, prayer leaders—any and all of these help the blood flow through the Body of Christ in the city. Yet, prayer is not the end itself, but a means to communicate with the Father, to become more like Christ, and to activate the Holy Spirit in our city. Jesus' model prayer in John 17 was for unity among His disciples "so the world may know" the Father had sent Jesus. As great as prayer movements are, they must serve the greater kingdom agenda of the reconciliation and restoration of all things in and under Christ's sovereignty.

Personally, I prefer to integrate prayer into activities we are already doing and will be doing, rather than making prayer the only activity. It is hard to gather people for a prayer-only meeting, but it is easy to add prayer to any other meeting or event. Pray with coffee or meal, pray before and after meetings, pray during worship events, pray in small groups, pray at large gatherings, pray with staff, pray at home, pray as you drive, etc.

Recently, I have made prayer during team meetings more focused by tying it to the purpose, mission, and outcomes of the team. For example, with our CityPartners team we ask the question, "Since our last meeting, how have we inspired people to love Hanoi, connected resources with opportunities, and/or networked people to form partnerships?" This results in testimonies and stories that otherwise may not surface. Then we solicit prayer requests from our partners and team members. This makes our praise and prayer time at the start of the meeting more meaningful and specific.

DON'T CALL THE MEETING TOO SOON: "Many times the quickest way to kill a partnership is to call a meeting—too soon!"[188] The mission is exciting, every Christian should join the effort, can't everyone see it? The fact is, most people cannot. Only 2.5% of people are innovators and 13.5% are early adopters. The early majority and the late majority are 34% each with another 16% lagging behind them.[189] At best, the early majority take time to deliberate before deciding to adopt a new idea, whereas the late majority will respond with caution and skepticism. The laggards look backwards, not forwards, and you may never get them on board. Therefore seek to partner with those who are venturesome and entrepreneurial, who have "the ability to understand and apply complex technical knowledge" and are comfortable "with a high degree of uncertainty."[190] Most likely, if you are reading this book, you are an innovator or early adopter yourself.

Westerners are often too focused on results, whereas Easterners and Southerners are focused on relationships (although they also love big loud events!). The Dutch have a saying, "To fall into the house with the door" ("*Met de deur in huis vallen*"), meaning going right to the point, being straight forward or direct. It took my wife a long time to train me to tone down my directness among Americans, and it took even longer to slow down enough to start conversations about the other person and their family's wellness. Relationships, trust, and creating buy-in takes time, so do not rush to call a meeting too soon, or chances are high that the majority will shut down your ideas before you even started!

THINK SKYSCRAPER, NOT HOTDOG STAND: Living in Hanoi, it seems that skyscrapers are popping up on every street corner every week. Obviously, that is not the case, but you can get the impression that building skyscrapers happen rather quickly. If you ever watched one go up from close by, you will have noticed how many months it takes just to dig and construct the foundation. After all, tens of floors with thousands of people will work and live on top of that foundation. Prior to that, months have been spent by developers, financers, architects, and engineers, to design the tower. The construction of the floors may seem to take only months, especially with steel and glass structures, but all in all, the project will have taken years—let alone the enormous amount of human and financial resources. In comparison, one person can set up a hotdog stand quickly and cheaply, but it takes a large team with lots of expertise and resources over a long period of time to plan, prepare, and execute the construction of a skyscraper.[191] In fact, a hotdog stand can be built for as little as $500,[192] whereas a skyscraper will more likely cost $500 million. (London's Shard started with a budget of $550 million but ended up costing four times as much. New York's One World Trade Center cost $3.9 billion, the most expensive in the world!)[193]

The point is clear: Launching and leading a citywide movement is more comparable to building a skyscraper (except the cost) than to setting up a hotdog stand (though we wish to do it on $500 only!). As the African proverb goes, "If you want to go fast, go alone. If you want to go far, go together." Citywide movements take a long time, a lot of resources, and a certain level of expertise to build. You cannot go at it alone; you must go together at a slower pace with the big picture in mind. One time I asked one of our Vietnamese Love in Action team members why he joined the team, because he seemed to love it yet not particularly interested in the details. "You seemed like a lonely soldier, so I joined to support you," was his honest answer (he could have been Dutch!). I came to the realization that I needed to work harder on recruiting, mobilizing, and empowering team members, because I cannot afford to come across as if I can do it all—because I cannot. Otherwise the project will turn out to be a hotdog stand, here today and gone tomorrow, instead of a skyscraper lasting beyond a century. (You might be interested to know that the Woolworth Building in New York City is the world's oldest skyscraper at 241meter / 792 feet tall, completed after three years in 1930.)[194]

SET LIMITED, ACHIEVABLE GOALS: Have you ever felt like you were "drinking from a firehose" when listening to a sermon or lecture? That is how other people feel when all you talk about is big ideas for far in the future. If the big vision is all you have, it will be quickly discouraging when only limited outcomes are achieved in the short run. Instead, consider the stages of transformation for setting limited, achievable goals to avoid disappointment.[195] "Quick wins" and "low hanging fruit" is what they are called. Easily accessible by all with a short time frame to complete.

Frequently I am told that I operate at the 10,000 meters/ 30,000 feet level most of the time and need to bring the vision down to ground level for people to see, understand, and engage with it. This does not come natural to me. Strengths Finder labels me as a Futurist, someone who is "inspired by the future and what could be [and] inspire others with their visions of the future."[196] A Futurist is someone who often says, "Wouldn't it be great if ..."[197] Futurists are visionaries who can see a detailed picture of future possibilities of the world, the organization, projects, products, or even other people, which is exciting for them and for others. Yet, Futurists must paint the picture for others vividly with such detail that they can see it too.

This is a great role for the catalyst of the citywide movement, which has been my privilege to fulfill. Following Clifton's advice, I need to allow myself more time to work out the details of that vision, share the vision with people who will appreciate it, brainstorm with another Futurist for increased heights and creativity, use metaphors, models, and images to describe the vision, break down the vision into actionable steps, and provide logical support to make it achievable. I also need people who are different from me, especially a "strong Activator" who "can transform innovative ideas into immediate action."[198]

A whole team of people is needed who are energized by the vision and ready to implement it. Others need this gift of future foresight as they do not have this vision of their own. Futurists cannot assume that others can see the same picture they see.[199] A false sense of humility will inhibit the Futurist from sharing their ideas or taking even more time to work out the details in vivid descriptions or assuming the lead. Time and again I run into the problem that I have not painted the picture vividly and clearly enough. As a result, people are left guessing what I am talking about. People also feel overwhelmed when I present the content of this whole book in a 90-minute seminar. I need an Activator to come alongside me to turn the big ideas into limited, achievable goals and, if you're a Futurist like me, you do too!

DEVELOP A ROAD MAP: "I want it done yesterday!" If not yesterday, then now, or at the latest, tomorrow. Visionaries want the future now, but that does not help anyone accomplish something. I have learned over the years that I can be off timewise, even if my vision was right. "I wanted this done last year," I have quipped more than once, as I can be off by years. The joy of working for decades in one city, though, is to see old ideas come to fruition, which many short-termers miss out on. The citywide movement leader needs to create a simple but clear list or diagram (or both) of action steps with names and deadlines so everyone is on the same page and knows what to expect.[200] This is why a diverse team is needed so everyone can play to their strengths.

In the framework of 5 Voices, this person is called a Pioneer. "With an unparalleled ability to think strategically, Pioneers are experts at aligning people, systems, and resources to deliver big-picture visions." They are a "can do" kind of people.[201] Though they cannot see as far as the Futurist, Pioneers prioritize vision, can make it sound compelling, and know how to create a step-by-step strategy to achieving that vision. Though they should not drive people too hard, or become defensive when their plans are questioned, Pioneers have a way to "align resource and people to make things happen."[202]

Since I am a visual person, I love diagrams! During sermon preparation, when I read words, I see pictures. I do not paint pictures with words but use pictures to find the right words to say. My PowerPoint presentation is done before I write any notes. People need to both see the picture and read or hear the words, which is why I like including lots of diagrams in this book. A basic action plan can be as simple as a list of steps with the names of people responsible and the deadline (see an example in Appendix A). For more complex processes and projects, a Gantt chart, flowchart, mind map, or other diagrams are more useful. Do an online search for "project plan template" and you will find plenty examples.[ac]

REMEMBER YOUR FOUR CONSTITUENCIES: The concept of the four constituencies which a partnership serves is very helpful to avoid treating everyone the same or forgetting one or more of the segments. The four constituencies are: the recipients of the ministry, the partner organizations and leaders, the supporters who pray and give, and the people in the partnership or network.[203] As Butler says, "Each of

---

[ac]   Check out venngage.com for free templates

these constituencies has hopes, expectations, and unique communication needs."[204] To avoid disappointment among each of these groupings, good communication is needed. A cycle of communication that not only shares needs but also reports on outcomes motivates everyone. You may need to add a public constituency to the four, depending how much you need to communicate differently to city government, citizens, and peer networks.

Segmenting your database or newsletter list is the simplest way to communicate with each of these groups. You may have one newsletter, but different introductions to the newsletter for each constituency. A communications coordinator would be a valuable addition to your team who can pay attention to each segment and stay on top of your communication cycle. Figuring out a communication strategy that is integrated with your cyclical project process is key. Having every team member informed and empowered to collect data, keep notes, take photos, shoot videos, and write reports will help you create the newsletters constituents want to read.

EXPECT CONFLICT: "Joy in Gospel Partnership" is the theme of Paul's letter to the Philippian church. The first congregation established on the European continent, the Philippian believers were faithful in supporting Paul's ministry, even while in prison. Yet, they had a problem perhaps every church has faced since then: interpersonal conflict. In Corinth, Christians had even gone to public court and Paul was trying to avoid that in Philippi. In chapter 4 of his letter, he names the two ladies who could not get along, treating both equally and respectfully as coworkers (*synergos* in Greek), and calls on a third companion to help resolve the conflict (v. 2-3). Not surprising, really, that there was conflict, considering the diversity of the congregation and the context of prideful Roman culture. Paul admonished them: "Rejoice in the Lord always. I will say it again: Rejoice!" (v. 4)

"When people work together, count on it—there are going to be differences in style, theology, lifestyle, understanding, experience, ministry approach, personality, heritage and background, maturity, and motivation," says Butler.[205] "Be ready. Be positive. Be proactive in dealing with it. Don't procrastinate."[206] Personally, I tend to avoid conflict, as do most people. Over time, however, I have learned to heed Butler's advice to not get anxious, to keep hopeful, to deal with it quickly, and to overcome my hesitation. After several positive experiences, I have gained confidence that the Lord truly honors those who seek peace, which encourages me to be more proactive.

THERE IS NO "RIGHT" WAY: Before you get too excited about copying the Love Hanoi model, or become discouraged because it will not work like this in your city, just remember: "There is no 'right way' for a city initiative to begin or to be organized."[207] Many, if not most, of the principles will still apply, but your city has a different story, culture, climate, ethnicity, economy, and spirituality than any other city. There is not one way about it, you must find your own way. That process of exploration is exciting! Do not rush towards formation, but enjoy the research, getting to know your city's nooks and crannies, talking to a variety of people, and falling in love with your city. Genuine love is the best motivator for a Love [Your City] campaign.

As I shared in the story at the beginning of the book, I was frustrated that Hanoi, Vietnam is not Boulder, Colorado. I love visiting Colorado and my friend Eric Swanson in Boulder, but strangely enough I love Hanoi more! I have visited almost every capital in SE Asia, but I still prefer living in Hanoi. God opened doors that we thought were shut and made things possible that we could not have imagined—and this is just the beginning. Just start and see where God will lead you!

IT TAKES TIME: "Transformation is a process, not an event."[208] There is no shortcut. Seven years is a good time frame to get started. Building relationships and trust among the citywide church leaders and within the city's government takes a lot of time—unless these relationships are already in place. "Significant change occurs over time," Butler said,[209] but you can be on the lookout for opportunities that will give your movement a head start or a boost along the way. Yet, true transformation might take a lifetime or longer. In fact, if you can accomplish your vision by yourself in your lifetime, it is not big enough!

Being a visionary, I am tempted to always look forward and not back. I tend to forget recent accomplishments, completed projects, lives touched, goals met, successes and failures past. I must be intentional in celebrating success, reviewing history, and distilling best practices. My team and my constituencies need such times to look back and so do I. Since this is God's idea and a God-sized project, allow things to take place in God's timing as well. Pulling a plow through muddy fields is hard, as we often see in picturesque photos of Vietnam's countryside. Pulling a plow while being yoked with Jesus is light and easy—which was His whole point. Pushing and pulling at the yoke will only give you blisters (and ulcers). As Paul wrote, "Since we live by the Spirit, let us keep in step with the Spirit" (Galatians 5:25).

THE ROLE OF INTERNATIONAL AND AFFLUENT CHURCHES

Finally, a special word of encouragement to leaders and members of International Churches (ICs). If you are not familiar with ICs, these are not simply churches overseas, i.e. a church plant of your denomination in a foreign country or a branch of a franchise church multiplication strategy. They are also not ethno-centric churches who maintain their home culture, language, and traditions. ICs are also not called "international" to look more impressive, but actually are national. ICs "are those churches around the world that primarily serve people of various nationalities (expatriates) and church backgrounds living outside their passport (home) countries."[210] HIF, for example, has over 50 nationalities represented among the 600 or so people gathering for worship services, including nationals.

The Missional International Church Network (MICN) believes that ICs are strategically positioned for kingdom impact. If you lead or attend an IC and have a missional vision for your church, you may have asked yourself these questions:

- What is the role of the international church in a citywide movement?
- How can expatriate Christians help unite local churches?
- Can the affluent help the poor besides just giving money?
- With the high turnover, how can we sustain a Love [Your City] campaign?

The stream of expatriate Christians is part of what is known as *the global diaspora*. It is estimated that "there are now over 200 million international migrants, and over 700 million internally displaced people or close to 1 billion scattered peoples."[211] The Global Diaspora Network (GDN), under the direction of Joy Tira, calls upon the church to respond to this phenomenon. Tira outlines three ways for Christians and churches to get involved, by ministering *to, through* and *beyond* the diaspora.[212] GDN's framework is helpful to describe the various ministries of the IC and how they can strive to become bridge builders into the local community.

By reaching out to the expatriate and immigrant community, the church is ministering *to* the diaspora in our city. Mobilizing and equipping these expatriate members to be missional is ministering *through* the diaspora to fellow expatriates. When expatriate members become acquainted with culture and language, they can minister *beyond* the diaspora and build bridges with the local churches and their host city. As mentioned before, the unity amidst the diversity in an international church is a true testimony and encouragement to local churches.

Equipping expatriate Christians to serve the poor in the city immediately raises the issue: How can an affluent IC help without hurting? It is easy to fall into the trap of believing that, unless you move into the poor neighborhood and live like the poor, you cannot effectively help the poor. Viv Grigg offers a much broader perspective:

> Typical Christian responses of aid and community development, even when done brilliantly, affect only the micro-environment of the squatters' area ... The primary response of middle-class Christians (while not neglecting other issues) will probably be in the transformation of economic life, political life, government bureaucracy, and other structures of the city that perpetuate slum poverty. It will probably also be necessary to deal with international factors that increasingly loom as dominant forces in worldwide urban poverty.[213]

In *Cry of the Urban Poor,* Grigg offers his recommendations for middle-class and international elite Christians and Churches. "Middle-class professionals ... may effect change in the implementation and governing of the cities at an urban planning level," while "Christians in the international elite may change the macro-economic systems."[214] In speaking of the role of the affluent church, Grigg writes, "Far more important [than giving financial help] is giving personnel who can impart spiritual life and technical skills."[215] Still, it is valid to provide financial support for widows, orphans, refugees, seed capital, expansion capital, scholarships, and community leadership programs.[216] This is encouraging insight, coming from a founder of a global ministry placing missionaries in urban slums. Everyone has a role to play in serving the least, the last, and the lost—as long as everyone maintains their focus on contributing *to* society rather than just consuming *from* society. Creating a ministry in the IC like HIF's CityPartners, that connects its resources with opportunities to give and serve, helps IC members to be connected heart-to-heart with the needs of their host city.

Go Ahead: Dip Your Toes In!

When, after 40 years of wondering in the desert, the Israelites stood on Jordan's shores, the banks of the river had been flooded. None except Joshua and Caleb had experienced the parting of the Red Sea, they had only heard the stories. Someone had to go first, though, and dip their toes in the water to see if it would move, as God had promised. Here's what happened:

> *Yet as soon as the priests who carried the ark reached the Jordan and their feet touched the water's edge, the water from upstream stopped flowing. It piled up in a heap a great distance away, at a town called Adam in the vicinity of Zarethan, while the water flowing down to the Sea of the Arabah (that is, the Dead Sea) was completely cut off. So the people crossed over opposite Jericho. The priests who carried the ark of the covenant of the Lord stopped in the middle of the Jordan and stood on dry ground, while all Israel passed by until the whole nation had completed the crossing on dry ground.* (Joshua 3:15-17)

God had been waiting for the priests to dip their toes in before He would stop the water from flowing far upstream. This may also be the case for your Love [Your City] initiative. Someone must start, someone needs to begin praying and doing, and someone needs to dip their toes in the water for God to start acting. God's response may be far upstream, but before you know it the obstacles disappear, and the people can cross over guided by your leadership and example. Perhaps the reason you have read this book all the way to the end is because God is calling you to be part of such a citywide movement? Maybe to initiate a Love [Your City] campaign in your city, town, or community?

The five steps to citywide movements will help you get started. **Step 1: Principles** will help you develop a theological framework for the city and urban ministry. A theology of placemaking goes way back to the garden of Eden and reaches far ahead to the New Jerusalem, and we find ourselves somewhere in the middle or towards the end of the story. Seeking the shalom of the city takes place through the reconciliation and restoration of the kingdom on earth as it is in heaven.

Such well-rounded theology will lead you to **Step 2: Posture**. As the Spirit transforms your mind to know God's "good, pleasing and perfect will" (Romans 12:2), your posture towards the city, the community, and the poor will also become more like that of Christ (Philippians 2:5-8).

Step 3: Process shows you where to start and what is next. It will be tempting to shortcut the process or go in reverse order, but keep the missional cycle in mind, so you will be hopeful of the outcomes. Remember ABCD: work with the people, rather than doing things for them, and start with small seed projects that you can implement together and build upon.

This takes you to **Step 4: Partner**, when you collaborate across sectors and boundaries to build networks and develop partnerships. As most cities are ethnically diverse, if you work with foreigners and immigrants, or you are an expatriate yourself, cross-cultural partnerships and teamwork require additional skills but have the potential to be highly effective.

Finally, to start building momentum in **Step 5: People**, you need to utilize different methods of gathering people together to share the vision and create ownership. Knowing what type of leader and kinds of skills are needed during the various stages of growth will help you and your team to select the right leader for each stage. It might be you, it might be someone else, or it may be a rotation of leaders, but God will lead your team in the process. BGU's eight perspectives of Transformational Leadership provides a helpful framework for selecting and growing such leaders. Together with the Love [Your City] team, you can implement various methods of gathering people in small and large consultations.

I am so excited that you have picked up my book and read it all the way through! If you are considering starting a Love [Your City] campaign, or are in the process of a similar initiative, I would love to hear from you. Please visit my website **www.bloemberg.org** and feel free to contact me with questions or testimonies.

APPENDIX A

LOVE HANOI CONFERENCE
OPERATING PROCEDURES

Date and Time: Saturday 6 April, 13:30-16:00

Roles:

Overseer: Surveys:

MC: Design:

Translation: Media:

Registration: Sound:

Welcome team: Photos:

Host presenters: Journalist:

Timekeeper: Cleanup:

Speakers' gifts: Small group feedback:

Product sales: Conference slides:

Breaks/snacks:

Pre-event operations:

Date	Item	Person(s)	*Note*	✓
13/3	Draft flyer submitted			
13/3	Updated video script			
15/3	Final flyer sent			
15/3	Announcement video sent			
17/3	Flyers and video presented on Sunday			
29/3	Receive presentations for review			
03/4	Final deadline for presentations			

Event operations:

Time	Item	Person(s)	Note	✓
12:00	Lunch with volunteers		# volunteers for order	
12:30	Set up sales, décor, stage, registration, tables, etc.		Love Hanoi banners in lobby and on stage	
	Welcome guest speakers			
13:30	Open doors			
13:50	Welcome people into auditorium			
14:00	Word of welcome and intro			
14:10	Plenary #1		PPT file	
14:30	Plenary #2		PPT file	
14:45	Plenary #3		PPT file	
15:00	Plenary #4		PPT file	
15:15	Group photo		Collect question cards from audience for panel discussion	
15:20	Coffee break		Cleanup	
15:40	Welcome people into auditorium			
15:45	Panel discussion with presenters		Questions	
16:05	Thank Yous to presenters		Gifts	
15:10	Survey instructions		Free Love Hanoi stickers/pen when handed in	
16:15	Small group discussions		Guiding questions on screen; collect feedback from groups	
16:30	Clean up, reset auditorium			
17:00	Close doors			

APPENDIX B

LOVE HANOI CONFERENCE PRESENTER GUIDELINES

Thank you for taking the time to inspire others at our upcoming Love Hanoi conference. From your presentation, we are looking primarily for these things:

- The big picture of the current challenges and opportunities on a very specific urban issue in Hanoi today.
- What you and/or your organization are doing to address this issue or a new idea you want to pitch to the audience for consideration.

Simple steps on how people in the audience can respond, participate or contribute, both organizations (companies, NGOs, churches) and individuals/families. Here are some important instructions to follow as you prepare:

- Please find enclosed a template PowerPoint file you can use (we use the Roboto font, which is multi-lingual). If you use your own branded design, please be sure to keep the font to 32pt minimum and wide screen format.
- We will have both Vietnamese and foreigners attend, please prepare a Vietnamese version and an English version of your presentation and we will use two screens to project. If you need help with translation, please let us know.
- We'll have simultaneous translation over headphones, so if you are Vietnamese please just speak in Vietnamese. Please speak slowly and articulate well so that the translator can follow you. It is important you send your PPT and notes one week in advance for the translator to become familiar with the terminology.
- If you have video and/or photos to share, please be sure they are HD widescreen and with translated subtitles if spoken in English or Vietnamese.

- Please send your presentations to at media@hif.vn one week prior to the conference so he can test it, give you feedback, fix it, and line it up.
- Please come at 13:00 so we can connect and make sure all is set prior to the conference. We're starting at 13:30 at our auditorium, 17th floor, Detech Tower, 8c Ton That Thuyet, Hanoi.
- Please stick to your allotted time as previously requested so everyone can share as prepared and we can finish on time. There will be someone with signs showing how many minutes you still have left. (We will stick to the scheduled time, but do not like to interrupt your presentation when you run overtime.)

If you have any questions, please feel free to contact me directly. We very much look forward to having you present and inspire us!

APPENDIX C

LOVE HANOI CONFERENCE SURVEY

Please fill out this survey to receive a free "Love Hanoi" sticker!

1. How did you learn about this conference?
   - ❑ Facebook post
   - ❑ HIF bulletin/announcement
   - ❑ CityPartners email
   - ❑ Invited by a friend
   - ❑ Through my organization/church
   - ❑ Other: _____

2. What is the main reason you attended this conference?
   - ❑ Interested in topic and content
   - ❑ To learn for personal growth
   - ❑ Networking and meet new people
   - ❑ Other: _____

3. Which presentation(s) was most interesting or helpful?
   - ❑ Lan Huong, Viet Youth
   - ❑ Thomas Abbott, Care for Children
   - ❑ Ngoc Anh, Christian Education
   - ❑ Shawn, Child Obesity
   - ❑ Panel discussion

4. How satisfied are you with the conference?
   - ❑ Very Satisfied
   - ❑ Somewhat Satisfied
   - ❑ Neither satisfied nor dissatisfied
   - ❑ Somewhat Dissatisfied
   - ❑ Very Dissatisfied

5. As a result of today's conference, what action will you take next?

6. What topic(s) or speakers would you recommend for the next conference?

7. How can we improve the next conference?

Name: _____

Organization/Church: _____

Phone: _____

E-mail: _____

APPENDIX D

THREE-DAY CONSULTATION PROGRAM

The three-day consultation can be run over a weekend, which helps leaders working weekdays to participate, if pastors can take the Sunday afternoon or evening off. Otherwise, starting on a Thursday evening is also possible, costing perhaps one vacation day on the Friday. The program can be as follows:[217]

Friday Evening (three hours)

1. Present case studies prepared by the team (videos are best)
2. Worship time (singing, prayer)
3. Small group discussions (focused on outcomes):
    - What did they come to the consultation for?
    - What do they want to go home with?
4. Collect answers on sticky notes by categories and post on poster- or whiteboards, having several teams report back to the whole group
5. The urban issue categories will become the discussion points

Saturday Morning (three hours)

1. Presentations by keynote speakers on the signs of hope in the city (6 presenters, 10-15 minutes each, including government, nonprofit, business, and ministry leaders)
2. Small group discussions (focused on what is current):
    - Share the signs of hope for the city
    - Discuss the needs of the city

Saturday Afternoon (four hours)

1. Visit various model sites (split groups up to visit about three sites, needing a total of 15 or more sites)

2. Review each site visit with these reflection questions:[218]
    - What is unique about the context of this model?
    - What is the history, big idea, vision, and origin?
    - What is the actual program and where and how is it delivered?
    - How is this model organized and structured? When did they start becoming organized?
    - Who is the primary audience? Who do they actually reach?
    - What are the costs of this model? How do they pay for it?
    - What is the theological rationale for the model?
    - How does this model equip others so that it is sustainable?
    - What are the strengths and the limitations?
    - What is the transferable principle?
3. The day may be concluded with an optional social event

Sunday Afternoon/Evening (three hours)

1. Small group discussion (focused on what is possible):
    - What was observed during the site visits?
    - What needs to be done in the city?
    - Design a program addressing identified issues
    - Identify major barriers to implementation
    - Decide on action steps (new network, new partnerships?)
2. Collect reports, having several teams report back to the whole group
3. Closing talk by the consultant/organizer

BIBLIOGRAPHY

Adler, Nancy J. *International Dimensions of Organizational Behavior*. 4th ed. Cincinnati, OH: South-Western, 2002.

Albrecht, David, Herve Hocquard, and Philippe Papin. *Urban Development in Vietnam: The Rise of Local Authorities*. Paris, France: Agence Francaise de Developpement, 2010.

Altman, Irwin, and Martin M. Chemers. *Culture and Environment*. Environment and Behavior. Cambridge, UK: Cambridge University Press, 1984.

An Ninh Thu Do. "Security in Hanoi Better Than My Country." An Ninh Thu Do, http://www.anninhthudo.vn/Vi-binh-yen-cuoc-song/An-ninh-o-Ha-Noi-con-tot-hon-nuoc-toi/552894.antd.

Anderson, Chris. *Ted Talks : The Official Ted Guide to Public Speaking*. Boston: Houghton Mifflin Harcourt, 2016.

Bakke Graduate University. "Transformational Leadership Perspectives Taught at Bgu." Bakke Graduate University, https://www.bgu.edu/about/eight-transformational-leadership-perspectives-taught-bgu/.

Bakke, Lowell. "Introduction." Paper presented at the Overture 1, Manila, Philippines, 11 January 2014.

Bakke, Raymond J. *A Theology as Big as the City*. Downers Grove, IL: InterVasity Press, 1997.

Bakke, Raymond J., and Jon Sharpe. *Street Signs : A New Direction in Urban Ministry*. Birmingham, AL: New Hope Publishers, 2006.

Ban Tôn giáo Chính phủ. "60 Năm Ngành Quản Lý Nhà Nước Về Tôn Giáo Ở Việt Nam 1955 - 2015 [60 Years of State Management of Religion in Vietnam 1955 - 2015]." Ban Tôn giáo Chính phủ, http://btgcp.gov.vn/Plus.aspx/vi/News/38/0/153/0/7759/60_nam_Nganh_quan_ly_nha_nuoc_ve_ton_giao_o_Viet_Nam_1955_2015.

———. "Cơ Cấu Tổ Chức Của Ban Tôn Giáo Chính Phủ [the Organizational Structure of the Government Committee for Religious Affairs]." Ban Tôn giáo Chính phủ, http://btgcp.gov.vn/Plus.aspx/vi/News/38/0/153/0/1060/Co_cau_to_chuc_cua_Ban_Ton_giao_Chinh_phu.

———. "Quá Trình Xây Dựng Và Phát Triển Của Ban Tôn Giáo Chính Phủ - Bộ Nội Vụ [the Process of Development and Development of the Government Committee for Religious Affairs - Ministry of Home Affairs]." Ban Tôn giáo Chính phủ, http://btgcp.gov.vn/Plus.aspx/vi/News/38/0/260/0/1062/Qua_trinh_xay_dung_va_phat_trien_cua_Ban_Ton_giao_Chinh_phu_Bo_Noi_vu.

Barth, Glenn. *The Good City: Transformed Lives Transforming Communities.* Tallmadge, OH: S.D. Myers Publishing Services, 2010.

Bauman, Stephan, Wendy Wellman, and Megan Laughlin. "The Wealth of the Poor: Women and the Savings Movement in Africa." The Lausanne Movement, https://www.lausanne.org/content/the-wealth-of-the-poor-women-and-the-savings-movement-in-africa-2.

Beltran, Benigno. "Social Empowerment." Paper presented at the Overture 1, Manila, Philippines, 16 January 2014.

Beltran, Benigno P. *The Christology of the Inarticulate : An Inquiry into the Filipino Understanding of Jesus the Christ.* Manila: Divine Word Publications, 1987.

Bloemberg, Jacob. "In Pursuit of Peace: Biblical Theology: How the Doctrines of Creation, Fall, Redemption, and New Creation Fuel Christian Engagement in Society." In *Evangelical Protestant faith: Historical Milestones and and Current Trends.* Hanoi 2017.

Bloemberg, Jacob, Cindy Brewer, and Dave Peacock. "Reconciliation." In *MICN 2015 Conference.* Bangkok: MICN, 2015.

Bloemberg, Jacob, and Luke Chatelein. "Love in Action." Hanoi: Love Hanoi Festival, 2017.

Butler, Phil. *Well Connected: Releasing the Power and Restoring Hope through Kingdom Partnerships.* Waynesboro, GA: Authentic Media, 2005.

Buttinger, Joseph, William J. Duiker, Gerald C. Hickey, Neil L. Jamieson, William S. Turley, and Milton Edgeworth Osborne. "Vietnam." Encyclopædia Britannica, Inc., http://www.britannica.com/place/Vietnam.

Cadman, Grace Hazenburg. "The Call of Jesus for Indo-China." *The Alliance Weekly* (November 11 1916).

Chu, Raineer. "Exegeting the City." Paper presented at the Overture 1, Manila, Philippines, 16 January 2014.

Clifton, Don. "Strengths Insight and Action-Planning Guide." New York, NY 2016.

⸻. *Strengthsfinder 2.0.* New York, NY: Gallup Press, 2017.

Cộng Hòa Xã Hội Chủ Nghĩa Việt Nam. "Luật Tín Ngưỡng, Tôn Giáo." Hanoi: Cộng Hòa Xã Hội Chủ Nghĩa Việt Nam, 2016.

Cope, Landa L. *An Introduction to the Old Testament Template : Rediscovering God's Principles for Discipling Nations.* 2nd ed. Seattle, WA: YWAM Pub., 2011.

Corbett, Steve, and Brian Fikkert. *When Helping Hurts: How to Alleviate Poverty without Hurting the Poor-- and Yourself.* Chicago, IL: Moody Publishers, 2009.

Cunningham, Loren. "Transcript of Interview of Loren Cunningham on Original 7 Mountains Vision." Marketplace Leaders Ministries, http://www.7culturalmountains.org/apps/articles/default.asp?articleid=40087.

DiGregorio, Michael R. "Imagining Public Space in Crowded Hanoi." The Asia Foundation, https://asiafoundation.org/2016/10/26/ reimagining-public-space-crowded-hanoi/.

Ellul, Jacques. *The Meaning of the City*. Eugene, OR: Wipf & Stock, 1970.

Encyclopædia Britannica. "Hanoi." Encyclopædia Britannica, http://www.britannica. com/place/Hanoi.

Gener, Tim. "Filipino Theology." Paper presented at the Overture 1, Manila, Philippines, 16 January 2014.

Goldwyn, Meathead. "So You Want to Start a Business? Why Not a Hot Dog Stand?" AmazingRibs.com, https://amazingribs.com/barbecue-history-and-culture/ so-you-want-start-business-why-not-hot-dog-stand.

Gornik, Mark R. *To Live in Peace: Biblical Faith and the Changing Inner City*. Grand Rapids, MI: William B Eerdmans Publishing Company, 2002.

Green, Gary P, and Anna Haines. *Asset Building & Community Development*. Thousand Oaks, CA: SAGE Publishers, Inc., 2012.

Grigg, Viv. *Cry of the Urban Poor*. Monrovia, CA: MARC, 1992.

_____. Email, 17 June 2019.

Hanoi Bible College. "Roundtable "Protestant Faith in the World and Vietnam," December 4–5, 2017." Hanoi Bible College, http://www.hbc.edu.vn/ roundtable-4-5-12-2017/.

Hanoi Portal. "Sắp Xếp Lại Tổ Chức Bộ Máy Của Ban Tôn Giáo Thuộc Sở Nội Vụ [Reorganize the Apparatus of the Religion Committee of the Department of Home Affairs]." Hanoi Portal, http://hanoi.gov.vn/chidaodieuhanh/-/hn/ t0gZB5w6V7Wh/2807/44033/1/sap-xep-lai-to-chuc-bo-may-cua-ban-ton-giao-thuoc-so-noi-vu.html;jsessionid=Ac8h1qHZYncApd0aKSA8XMvx. app2.

Hattem, Julian. "Turning the World's Largest Refugee Camp into a City." Public Radio International, https://www.pri.org/stories/2017-09-22/ turning-worlds-largest-refugee-camp-big-city.

Hofstede, Geert. "The 6-D Model of National Culture." https://geerthofstede.com/ culture-geert-hofstede-gert-jan-hofstede/6d-model-of-national-culture/.

Hoitnick, Yvette. "Why the Little Dutch Boy Never Put His Finger in the Dike." Dutch Genealogy, https://www.dutchgenealogy.nl/ why-the-little-dutch-boy-never-put-his-finger-in-the-dike/.

Jones, E. Stanley. *Christ's Alternative to Communism*. New York: The Abingdon Press, 1935.

Joshua Project. "What Is the 10/40 Window?" U.S. Center for World Mission, http:// joshuaproject.net/resources/articles/10_40_window.

Kretzmann, John, and John McKnight. *Building Communities from the inside Out: A Path toward Finding an Mobilizing a Community's Assets*. Chicago, IL: ACTA Publications, 1993.

Kubicek, Jeremie, and Steve Cockram. *5 Voices*. Hoboken, NJ: John Wiley & Sons, Inc., 2016.

Linden, Russell Matthew. *Leading across Boundaries: Creating Collaborative Agencies in a Networked World*. 1st ed. San Francisco, CA: Jossey-Bass, 2010.

Linthicum, Robert. *City of God, City of Satan: A Biblical Theology of the Urban Church*. Grand Rapids, MI: Zondervan Publishing House, 1991.

Lupton, Robert D. *Renewing the City: Reflections on Community Development and Urban Renewal*. Downers Grove, IL: InterVarsity Press, 2005.

McClung, Floyd. *Living on the Devil's Doorstep: The Mcclung Family Story*. Waco, TX: Word Books, 1988.

McKnight, John, and John Kretzmann. "Mapping Community Capacity." Institute for Policy Research, 1996.

Missio Nexus. "The Great Commission: Big & Important!" Missio Nexus, https://missionexus.org/the-great-commission-big-important/.

_____. "Think Big, Think Small: Partnerships as a Revolution in Global Missions." Missio Nexus, https://missionexus.org/think-big-think-small-partnerships-as-a-revolution-in-global-missions/.

Moffit, Bob. "Seeds and Seed Projects." (2007).

Murray, Don. "The Cross and the Switchblade." Harlem: Gateway Productions, 1970.

Myers, Bryant L. *Walking with the Poor: Principles and Practices of Transformational Development*. Maryknoll, NY: Orbix Books, 2011.

Nguyen, Phuc Vinh. *Hanoi Past and Present*. Hanoi: The Gioi Publishers, 2004.

Price-Thomas, Steven. 23 February 2016.

Reimer, Johannes. "Community Transformation, Peace and Church Growth." Micah/PRN Global Series, 2019.

_____. "Love Hanoi Conference." Hanoi 2013.

Reimer, Reg. *Vietnam's Christians: Century of Growth in Adversity*. Pasadena, CA: William Carey Library, 2011.

Rickett, Daniel. *Building Strategic Relationships: A Practical Guide to Partnering with Non-Western Missions*. Updated. ed. Minneapolis, MI: STEM Press, 2003.

_____. *Making Your Partnership Work*. Enumclaw, WA: WinePress Pub., 2002.

Roberts, Bob. *Glocalization: How Followers of Jesus Engage the New Flat World*. Grand Rapids, MI: Zondervan, 2007.

Rogers, Everett M. *Diffusion of Innovations*. 5th ed. New York: Free Press, 2003.

Smith, T. Aaron. *Living in the Neighborhood: Developing a Sustainable Incarnational Ministry among the Urban Poor*. Pomona, CA: Servant Partners, 2013.

Sparks, Paul, Tim Sorens, and Dwight J. Friesen. *The New Parish: How Neighborhood Churches Are Transforming Mission, Discipleship and Community*. Downers Grove, IL: InterVarsity Press, 2014.

Spees, H. P. "Peace for the Cities: Building a Global Christ-Centered Civic Renewal Movement for the Twenty-First Century." Seattle, WA, 2012.

Stott, Rory. "These Are the World's Most Expensive Skyscrapers." HuffPost Entertainment, https://www.huffpost.com/entry/most-expensive-skyscraper_n_6278832.

Swanson, Eric, and Sam Williams. *To Transform a City: Whole Church, Whole Gospel, Whole City.* Grand Rapids, MI: Zondervan, 2010.

Sweney, Chip. *A New Kind of Big: How Churches of Any Size Can Partner to Transform Communities.* Grand Rapids, MI: Baker Books, 2011.

Tira, Sadiri Joy, ed. *The Human Tidal Wave.* Pasig City, Philippines: Lifechange Publishing, Inc., 2013.

Tuoi Tre News. "Vietnam Deputy Pm Appointed Secretary of Hanoi Party Committee." Tuoi Tre News, http://tuoitrenews.vn/politics/33158/vietnam-deputy-pm-appointed-secretary-of-hanoi-party-committee.

Unite! "Unite!" http://www.uniteus.org/.

Van Eymeren, Andre. "Creating Shalom in the City: A Roadmap for Human Flourishing." In *Urban Shalom & the Cities We Need*, edited by Andre Van Eymeren, Ash Barker, Bryan McCabe and Chris Elisara. Birmingham: Urban Shalom Publishing, 2017.

Van Eymeren, Andre, Ash Barker, Bryan McCabe, and Chris Elisara. *Urban Shalom & the Cities We Need.* Birmingham: Urban Shalom Publishing, 2017.

VNS. "Hanoi's Population Breaks Forecast for 2030." DTI News, http://dtinews.vn/en/news/017004/59093/hanoi-s-population-breaks-forecast-for-2030.html.

Vu, Hien. "Hanoi Reformation Anniversary Roundtable Summary." Washington D.C.: Institute for Global Engagement, 2017.

Wikipedia. "World Population Estimates." Wikipedia, https://en.wikipedia.org/wiki/World_population_estimates#Cumulative_population.

World Bank Group, and Ministry of Planning and Investment of Vietnam. *Vietnam 2035: Toward Prosperity, Creativity, Equity, and Democracy.* Washington, DC: World Bank Group, 2016.

World Food Program USA. "Rohingya Crisis: A First Look into the World's Largest Refugee Camp." World Food Program USA, https://www.wfpusa.org/stories/rohingya-crisis-a-firsthand-look-into-the-worlds-largest-refugee-camp/.

Zaheer, Sidrah. "Top 10 Oldest Skyscrapers in the World." Gizmocrazed, https://www.gizmocrazed.com/2012/06/top-10-oldest-skyscrapers-in-the-world/.

NOTES

1   Don Murray, "The Cross and the Switchblade," (Harlem: Gateway Productions, 1970).

2   Floyd McClung, *Living on the Devil's Doorstep: The Mcclung Family Story* (Waco, TX: Word Books, 1988).

3   Joshua Project, "What Is the 10/40 Window?," U.S. Center for World Mission, http://joshuaproject.net/resources/articles/10_40_window.

4   Eric Swanson and Sam Williams, *To Transform a City: Whole Church, Whole Gospel, Whole City* (Grand Rapids, MI: Zondervan, 2010), 15.

5   An Ninh Thu Do, "Security in Hanoi Better Than My Country," An Ninh Thu Do, http://www.anninhthudo.vn/Vi-binh-yen-cuoc-song/An-ninh-o-Ha-Noi-con-tot-hon-nuoc-toi/552894.antd.

6   Jacob Bloemberg, "In Pursuit of Peace: Biblical Theology: How the Doctrines of Creation, Fall, Redemption, and New Creation Fuel Christian Engagement in Society," in *Evangelical Protestant faith: Historical Milestones and and Current Trends* (Hanoi 2017).

7   Joseph Buttinger et al., "Vietnam," Encyclopædia Britannica, Inc., http://www.britannica.com/place/Vietnam.

8   Encyclopædia Britannica, "Hanoi," Encyclopædia Britannica, http://www.britannica.com/place/Hanoi.

9   Phuc Vinh Nguyen, *Hanoi Past and Present* (Hanoi: The Gioi Publishers, 2004), 45.

10 Encyclopædia Britannica.

11 Ibid.

12 Ibid.

13 Nguyen, 63-64.

14 Encyclopædia Britannica.

15 World Bank Group and Ministry of Planning and Investment of Vietnam, *Vietnam 2035: Toward Prosperity, Creativity, Equity, and Democracy* (Washington, DC: World Bank Group, 2016), 79.

16 Nguyen, 94.

17 World Bank Group and Ministry of Planning and Investment of Vietnam, 88.

18 Steven Price-Thomas, 23 February 2016.

19 World Bank Group and Ministry of Planning and Investment of Vietnam, 77-78.

20 David Albrecht, Herve Hocquard, and Philippe Papin, *Urban Development in Vietnam: The Rise of Local Authorities* (Paris, France: Agence Francaise de Developpement, 2010), 18.

21 Adapted from ibid., 19.

22 Tuoi Tre News, "Vietnam Deputy Pm Appointed Secretary of Hanoi Party Committee," Tuoi Tre News, http://tuoitrenews.vn/politics/33158/vietnam-deputy-pm-appointed-secretary-of-hanoi-party-committee.

23 Hanoi Portal, "Sắp Xếp Lại Tổ Chức Bộ Máy Của Ban Tôn Giáo Thuộc Sở Nội Vụ [Reorganize the Apparatus of the Religion Committee of the Department of Home Affairs]," Hanoi Portal, http://hanoi.gov.vn/chidaodieuhanh/-/hn/t0gZB5w6V7Wh/2807/44033/1/sap-xep-lai-to-chuc-bo-may-cua-ban-ton-giao-thuoc-so-noi-vu.html;jsessionid=Ac8h1qHZYncApd0aKSA8XMvx.app2.

24 Ban Tôn giáo Chính phủ, "Cơ Cấu Tổ Chức Của Ban Tôn Giáo Chính Phủ [the Organizational Structure of the Government Committee for Religious Affairs]," Ban Tôn giáo Chính phủ, http://btgcp.gov.vn/Plus.aspx/vi/News/38/0/153/0/1060/Co_cau_to_chuc_cua_Ban_Ton_giao_Chinh_phu.

25 Cộng Hòa Xã Hội Chủ Nghĩa Việt Nam, "Luật Tín Ngưỡng, Tôn Giáo," (Hanoi: Cộng Hòa Xã Hội Chủ Nghĩa Việt Nam, 2016), 1.

26 Ibid.

27 Ibid., 2.

28 Ibid., 4.

29 Ibid., 11.

30 Ibid.

31 Ibid., 16.

32 Ibid., 18-21.

33 Ibid., 23.

34 Ibid., 24.

35 Ibid., 25.

36 Ibid., 29-30.

37 Reg Reimer, *Vietnam's Christians: Century of Growth in Adversity* (Pasadena, CA: William Carey Library, 2011).

38 Ibid., 38.

39 Ibid., 52.

40 Ibid., 26.

41 Ibid., 27.

42 Grace Hazenburg Cadman, "The Call of Jesus for Indo-China," *The Alliance Weekly* (1916): 91.

43 Reimer, 30.

44 Ibid., 28-29.

45 Ibid., 40.

46 Ibid., 41.

47 Cadman.

48 Reimer, 41.

49 Ibid., 106.

50 Ibid., 72.

51   Ibid., 69.

52   Ibid., 72.

53   Ibid.

54   Raymond J Bakke, *A Theology as Big as the City* (Downers Grove, IL: InterVasity Press, 1997), 30.

55   Irwin Altman and Martin M. Chemers, *Culture and Environment*, Environment and Behavior (Cambridge, UK: Cambridge University Press, 1984), 217.

56   Jacques Ellul, *The Meaning of the City* (Eugene, OR: Wipf & Stock, 1970), 10.

57   Wikipedia, "World Population Estimates," Wikipedia, https://en.wikipedia.org/wiki/World_population_estimates#Cumulative_population. Accessed on March 30, 2019

58   Bryant L Myers, *Walking with the Poor: Principles and Practices of Transformational Development* (Maryknoll, NY: Orbix Books, 2011), 97.

59   Ibid.

60   Ibid., 98.

61   Ibid.

62   Ibid., 181.

63   Andre Van Eymeren et al., *Urban Shalom & the Cities We Need* (Birmingham: Urban Shalom Publishing, 2017), 16.

64   World Food Program USA, "Rohingya Crisis: A First Look into the World's Largest Refugee Camp," World Food Program USA, https://www.wfpusa.org/stories/rohingya-crisis-a-firsthand-look-into-the-worlds-largest-refugee-camp/. Accessed on March 30, 2019

65   Julian Hattem, "Turning the World's Largest Refugee Camp into a City," Public Radio International, https://www.pri.org/stories/2017-09-22/turning-worlds-largest-refugee-camp-big-city. Accessed on March 30, 2019

66   Michael R. DiGregorio, "Imagining Public Space in Crowded Hanoi," The Asia Foundation, https://asiafoundation.org/2016/10/26/reimagining-public-space-crowded-hanoi/. Accessed on March 30, 2019

67   Bakke, 86-87.

68   Johannes Reimer, "Community Transformation, Peace and Church Growth," (Micah/PRN Global Series, 2019), 7-8.

69   E. Stanley Jones, *Christ's Alternative to Communism* (New York: The Abingdon Press, 1935), 29.

70   Swanson and Williams.

71   Yvette Hoitnick, "Why the Little Dutch Boy Never Put His Finger in the Dike," Dutch Genealogy, https://www.dutchgenealogy.nl/why-the-little-dutch-boy-never-put-his-finger-in-the-dike/. Accessed on March 30, 2019

72   See Swanson and Williams. See also Landa L. Cope, *An Introduction to the Old Testament Template : Rediscovering God's Principles for Discipling Nations*, 2nd ed. (Seattle, WA: YWAM Pub., 2011).

73 Adapted from H. P. Spees, "Peace for the Cities: Building a Global Christ-Centered Civic Renewal Movement for the Twenty-First Century," (Seattle, WA 2012).

74 Adapted from ibid.

75 Adapted from ibid.

76 Ibid., 146-48.

77 Adapted from ibid.

78 Ibid.

79 Adapted from ibid.

80 Ibid. Italics mine.

81 Ibid.

82 Ibid.

83 Benigno Beltran, "Social Empowerment" (paper presented at the Overture 1, Manila, Philippines, 16 January 2014).

84 Benigno P. Beltran, *The Christology of the Inarticulate: An Inquiry into the Filipino Understanding of Jesus the Christ* (Manila: Divine Word Publications, 1987).

85 Beltran.

86 Lowell Bakke, "Introduction" (ibid.11 January).

87 Raineer Chu, "Exegeting the City" (ibid.16 January).

88 Ibid.

89 Adapted from Ibid.

90 Paul Sparks, Tim Sorens, and Dwight J. Friesen, *The New Parish: How Neighborhood Churches Are Transforming Mission, Discipleship and Community* (Downers Grove, IL: InterVarsity Press, 2014), 23.

91 Ibid., 24.

92 Ibid., 31.

93 Ibid., 23.

94 Ibid., 149.

95 Steve Corbett and Brian Fikkert, *When Helping Hurts: How to Alleviate Poverty without Hurting the Poor-- and Yourself* (Chicago, IL: Moody Publishers, 2009), 30.

96 Ibid., 61.

97 Ibid., 62. Quoting Bryant Myers, author of *Walking with the Poor*.

98 Ibid., 185.

99 Ibid., 64.

100 Myers, 145.

101 Stephan Bauman, Wendy Wellman, and Megan Laughlin, "The Wealth of the Poor: Women and the Savings Movement in Africa," The Lausanne Movement, https://www.lausanne.org/content/the-wealth-of-the-poor-women-and-the-savings-movement-in-africa-2.

102 Corbett and Fikkert, 69.

103 Myers, 148.

104 T. Aaron Smith, *Living in the Neighborhood: Developing a Sustainable Incarnational Ministry among the Urban Poor* (Pomona, CA: Servant Partners, 2013).

105 Mark R Gornik, *To Live in Peace: Biblical Faith and the Changing Inner City* (Grand Rapids, MI: William B Eerdmans Publishing Company, 2002), 132-33.

106 For other outlines and retelling of Nehemiah: Robert D. Lupton, *Renewing the City: Reflections on Community Development and Urban Renewal* (Downers Grove, IL: InterVarsity Press, 2005). *City of God, City of Satan: A Biblical Theology of the Urban Church* (Grand Rapids, MI: Zondervan Publishing House, 1991).

107 Adapted from Gornik, 133-45.

108 Adapted from Johannes Reimer, "Love Hanoi Conference," (Hanoi 2013).

109 Adapted from Johannes Reimer, "Community Transformation, Peace and Church Growth," 28.

110 Adapted from ibid., 29.

111 Gornik, 173.

112 Ibid., 174.

113 John Kretzmann and John McKnight, *Building Communities from the inside Out: A Path toward Finding an Mobilizing a Community's Assets* (Chicago, IL: ACTA Publications, 1993), 346.

114 Ibid., 18.

115 Adapted from John McKnight and John Kretzmann, "Mapping Community Capacity," (Institute for Policy Research, 1996), 21.

116 Adapted from Kretzmann and McKnight, 30-31.

117 Adapted from ibid., 34.

118 Adapted from ibid., 44.

119 Adapted from ibid., 158.

120 Ibid., chapter 4.

121 Ibid., 353.

122 Myers, 151.

123 Ibid., 195.

124 Gary P Green and Anna Haines, *Asset Building & Community Development* (Thousand Oaks, CA: SAGE Publishers, Inc., 2012), 117.

125 Ibid., 144.

126 Ibid., 159.

127 Ibid., 189.

128 Ibid., 213.

129 Ibid., 239.

130 Ibid., 255.

131 Swanson and Williams, 99.

132 Daniel Rickett, *Building Strategic Relationships: A Practical Guide to Partnering with Non-Western Missions*, Updated. ed. (Minneapolis, MI: STEM Press, 2003), 13,15.

133 Chip Sweney, *A New Kind of Big: How Churches of Any Size Can Partner to Transform Communities* (Grand Rapids, MI: Baker Books, 2011).

134 Ibid., 15.

135 Interview by Jacob Bloemberg, 2016.

136 Phil Butler, *Well Connected: Releasing the Power and Restoring Hope through Kingdom Partnerships* (Waynesboro, GA: Authentic Media, 2005), 261.

137 Adapted from ibid., 277.

138 Loren Cunningham, "Transcript of Interview of Loren Cunningham on Original 7 Mountains Vision," Marketplace Leaders Ministries, http://www.7culturalmountains.org/apps/articles/default.asp?articleid=40087.

139 Bob Roberts, *Glocalization: How Followers of Jesus Engage the New Flat World* (Grand Rapids, MI: Zondervan, 2007), 41.

140 Russell Matthew Linden, *Leading across Boundaries: Creating Collaborative Agencies in a Networked World*, 1st ed. (San Francisco, CA: Jossey-Bass, 2010), 1.

141 Adapted from ibid., 267-73.

142 Adapted from Daniel Rickett, *Making Your Partnership Work* (Enumclaw, WA: WinePress Pub., 2002), 21.

143 Adapted from ibid., 20-22.

144 Adapted from ibid., 38.

145 Ibid., 36.

146 Nancy J. Adler, *International Dimensions of Organizational Behavior*, 4th ed. (Cincinnati, OH: South-Western, 2002), 148.

147 Ibid., 149.

148 Rickett, *Building Strategic Relationships: A Practical Guide to Partnering with Non-Western Missions*, 39.

149 Geert Hofstede, "The 6-D Model of National Culture," https://geerthofstede.com/culture-geert-hofstede-gert-jan-hofstede/6d-model-of-national-culture/.

150 (Adler, 2002, 184)

151 Missio Nexus, "The Great Commission: Big & Important!," Missio Nexus, https://missionexus.org/the-great-commission-big-important/.

152 Butler, 202.

153 Glenn Barth, *The Good City: Transformed Lives Transforming Communities* (Tallmadge, OH: S.D. Myers Publishing Services, 2010).

154 Adapted from ibid., 41.

155 Raymond J. Bakke and Jon Sharpe, *Street Signs : A New Direction in Urban Ministry* (Birmingham, AL: New Hope Publishers, 2006), 227.

156 Barth, 41.

157 Butler, 124.

158 Barth, 49.

159 Adapted from Swanson and Williams, 179.

160 Adapted from Ibid., 182.

161 Barth, 52-58.

162 Global Net Productions, 1999, 2002

163 Barth, 59-61.

164 Adapted from Bakke Graduate University, "Transformational Leadership Perspectives Taught at Bgu," Bakke Graduate University, https://www.bgu.edu/about/eight-transformational-leadership-perspectives-taught-bgu/.

165 Viv Grigg, Email, 17 June 2019.

166 Bakke Graduate University.

167 Tim Gener, "Filipino Theology" (paper presented at the Overture 1, Manila, Philippines, 16 January 2014).

168 Bakke Graduate University.

169 Jacob Bloemberg, Cindy Brewer, and Dave Peacock, "Reconciliation," in *MICN 2015 Conference* (Bangkok: MICN, 2015).

170 Bakke and Sharpe, 139.

171 Ibid., 139-40.

172 Ibid., 142.

173 Adapted from ibid., 131-44.

174 Chris Anderson, *Ted Talks : The Official Ted Guide to Public Speaking* (Boston: Houghton Mifflin Harcourt, 2016).

175 Swanson and Williams, 17.

176 Spees, 29-30.

177 Bakke and Sharpe, 254.

178 For more information, visit http://www.thinktankinitiative.org/blog/think-tanks-sign-santiago-declaration-sustainable-development-goals-1

179 Bakke and Sharpe, 256.

180 Butler, 33.

181 Ibid., 138.

182 Ibid., 287.

183 Ibid., 50.

184 Ibid., 95.

185 Missio Nexus.

186 "Think Big, Think Small: Partnerships as a Revolution in Global Missions," Missio Nexus, https://missionexus.org/think-big-think-small-partnerships-as-a-revolution-in-global-missions/.

187 Butler, 110.

188 Ibid., 112.

189 Everett M. Rogers, *Diffusion of Innovations*, 5th ed. (New York: Free Press, 2003), 281.

190 Ibid., 282-85.

191 Butler, 115.

192 Meathead Goldwyn, "So You Want to Start a Business? Why Not a Hot Dog Stand?," AmazingRibs.com, https://amazingribs.com/barbecue-history-and-culture/so-you-want-start-business-why-not-hot-dog-stand. Accessed on September 13, 2019.

193 Rory Stott, "These Are the World's Most Expensive Skyscrapers," HuffPost Entertainment, https://www.huffpost.com/entry/most-expensive-skyscraper_n_6278832. Accessed on September 13, 2019.

194 Sidrah Zaheer, "Top 10 Oldest Skyscrapers in the World," Gizmocrazed, https://www.gizmocrazed.com/2012/06/top-10-oldest-skyscrapers-in-the-world/. Accessed on June 26, 2019.

195 Butler, 158.

196 Don Clifton, "Strengths Insight and Action-Planning Guide," (New York, NY 2016), 4.

197 *Strengthsfinder 2.0* (New York, NY: Gallup Press, 2017), 105.

198 Ibid., 107,43.

199 Ibid., 106-08.

200 Ibid., 181-82.

201 Jeremie Kubicek and Steve Cockram, *5 Voices* (Hoboken, NJ: John Wiley & Sons, Inc., 2016), 40.

202 Ibid., 41-42.

203 Butler, 189.

204 Ibid., 221.

205 Ibid., 193.

206 Ibid., 196.

207 Ibid., 282.

208 Ibid., 288.

209 Ibid., 63.

210 MICN, "What Is an IC?" MICN, http://micn.org/.

211 Sadiri Joy Tira, ed. *The Human Tidal Wave* (Pasig City, Philippines: Lifechange Publishing, Inc., 2013), xxi.

212 Ibid., 163.

213 Viv Grigg, *Cry of the Urban Poor* (Monrovia, CA: MARC, 1992), 262-63.

214 Ibid., 263.

215 Ibid., 283.

216 Ibid., 283-84.

217 Adapted from Bakke and Sharpe, 279-80.

218 Ibid., 250.

Jacob Bloemberg moved with his family to Hanoi, Vietnam in 1997 to work at children's homes. In 2005 he became the Lead Pastor of Hanoi International Fellowship with a vision to turn the church inside-out. HIF launched the Love Hanoi campaign in 2012, which over the years has become a citywide movement. Their Love Hanoi story is inspiring Christian leaders around the world to start their own *Love [Your City]* campaigns in their cities.

Jacob holds a Doctorate in Transformational Leadership: City Transformation from Bakke Graduate University and is ordained under Elim Fellowship, NY. He has been a member of the International Leadership Team of the Missional International Church Network since 2005. Jacob is of Dutch nationality and his wife Linda hails from Pennsylvania, USA. Their three adult children grew up in Hanoi and now live in three different continents.

For more information, articles, book reviews, and tools, visit:

www.bloemberg.org